STRENGTH —of— SOUL

The Sacred Use of Time

Books by W. Philip Keller:

Splendor from the Sea
As a Tree Grows
Bold under God—A Fond Look at a Frontier Preacher
A Shepherd Looks at Psalm 23
A Layman Looks at the Lord's Prayer
Rabboni—Which is to say, Master
A Shepherd Looks at the Good Shepherd and His Sheep
A Gardener Looks at the Fruits of the Spirit
Mighty Man of Valor—Gideon
Mountain Splendor
Taming Tension
Expendable
Still Waters
A Child Looks at Psalm 23
Ocean Glory
Walking with God
On Wilderness Trails
Elijah—Prophet of Power
Salt for Society
A Layman Looks at the Lamb of God
Lessons from a Sheep Dog
Wonder O' the Wind
Joshua—Mighty Warrior and Man of Faith
A Layman Looks at the Love of God
Sea Edge
David I
David II
Sky Edge
Chosen Vessels
In the Master's Hands
Predators in Our Pulpits
Songs of My Soul
Thank You, Father
God Is My Delight
Pleasures Forevermore
Strength of Soul

W. PHILLIP KELLER

Author of *A Shepherd Looks at Psalm 23*

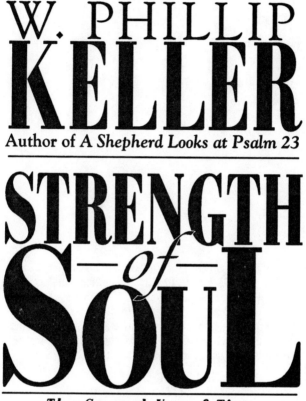

STRENGTH —*of*— SOUL

The Sacred Use of Time

kregel
PUBLICATIONS

Grand Rapids, MI 49501

Cover photo: © W. Phillip Keller
Cover and book design: Alan G. Hartman

Library of Congress Cataloging-in-Publication Data

Keller, W. Phillip (Weldon Phillip), 1920-

Strength of soul: the sacred use of time / W. Phillip Keller.
    p.   cm.
    1. Christian life—1960-   . 2. Time management—Religious aspects—Christianity. I. Title.
BV4501.2.K4258   1993   248.4—dc20   92-43992
                                        CIP

ISBN 0-8254-2997-8

1 2 3 4 5 6 Printing/Year 97 96 95 94 93

Printed in the United States of America

To "Bernie"

My Dearly Loved Friend,
Also Dearly Loved by Our Father

CONTENTS

With Genuine Gratitude

This has been a challenging work that called for courage and endurance to write throughout an unusually ferocious, summer season. Morning by morning the intense awareness of my Father's strength, wisdom and care enabled me to carry on.

The interest, love and prayers of precious people scattered across the country and close at hand are a heartening encouragement. Some have prayed for me for years and years. What a blessing!

The genuine enthusiasm and quiet efficiency of Al Bryant, my editor and friend, are rare and special. Together we have worked on many manuscripts across the years, with pleasure.

And a special word of thanks goes to Fern Webber who typed the work. She has the remarkable ability to read my hand-written pages and turn them into a splendid manuscript. She is a gift from our Father in this endeavor.

Blessings and best wishes to each of you.

To All Who Read This

Strength of Soul is the supreme secret to successful living.
Without it our days are difficult and drab.

Inner serenity brings strength of character,
strength of soul,
sturdiness of personality.

Without it we are easily dismayed,
readily swayed by events around us.

Strength of Soul injects joy and enthusiasm into life.
Lacking it, we drift without direction.

It injects an element of delight into our advancing years.
There truly is *Strength of Soul* for those who seek it.

In sincerity I ask you, the reader,
to contemplate these chapters with care.

Please read these pages slowly, slowly, to relish and
reflect, and to come to know the living Christ.

1

COMING TO TERMS WITH TIME

T ime is a treasure.

Time is the unique opportunity given each of us to do something beautiful, noble and worthwhile.

Time, though transient, enables a person to create that which will endure.

Time is the lovely gift from God, our Father, that allows us to relish life.

Each new day is an untouched, uncut gem placed in my possession to shape and polish. What will I do with it?

When we have completed a week, a month, a year or even a lifetime it is possible to look upon a string of polished jewels. Each interval of time bears its own special facet of splendor, its inner glory of serenity, its strength of soul.

This is doubly so if I allow Christ to control my time. He has His own wonderful ways of bringing unusual beauty into each of my days. He can arrange my hours so that they sparkle with pleasure.

Much of this depends upon whether or not I have His perspective on the passing scene around me. Do I really "see" the brilliant yellow blooms of the sturdy "*Johnny Jump-ups*" that burst from the barren clay after the first winter rains? Do I really "see" the sea gulls soaring in wild abandon above the wind-driven surf? Do I really "see" and give humble thanks for the gentle smile of a stranger?

What do I do with this gift of time, entrusted so tenderly to my care? Should I waste it on worry and fretting? Or will I learn to fling myself happily into my Father's warm embrace, and whisper softly, "Oh my Beloved, I am in Your care. Lead me gently to see life through Your eyes today." Then it will be a treasure!

Time is more, much more than something to be spent. We speak glibly of "*spending time.*" It is far, far too precious to pass off in idle, empty pursuits, which means it is actually squandered—thrown away—never, ever to be retrieved. Rather, it is to be savored, relished, cherished with care.

The profound, searching, eloquent question is, each new dawn, "*What will be done with this day?*" It is a unique and special opportunity, an interval of eternity, in which the intense essence of life itself can be distilled from the moment.

It is not a question of "*filling in time.*" It is a matter of how can this interlude fill my soul, enrich my spirit, nourish my well being as well as the lives of others around me? Can these hours be spent wisely and well? Can they be a benediction and not a burden? Can they lend strength to my soul and others?

For those of us who treasure our time there really are endless ways in which we can invest our time in others—to their advantage as well as ours. Yesterday was a case in point. I awoke early to find a heavy blanket of snow had covered the landscape during the night. It would be difficult for most older people to get around. Most of them would feel "trapped" in their lodgings. Never mind the difficult driving, the dangerous ice, I decided to go and visit a solitary old sailor in a nearby village. When I came to his door he broke into broad smiles. The loneliness of an otherwise long, long day had been dispelled by my arrival.

We sat in the soft, mellow glow of lamplight while he re-lived the stirring interludes of his adventures along the coast. His handsome cat curled up on my lap as if to say, "This is doing the *boss* a world of good!"

He is a huge man, with enormous shoulders and the great strong hands of a seaman who has handled rigging and ropes and sails in heavy "blows." Yet within that mighty frame resides the gentle soul of one who has come to love Christ with quiet faith. It was not always so. In his youth he had been rough and tough. But now we spoke gently of "Our Friend," whose care and companionship have made it possible for his twilight years to be lived out in dignity.

I watched the mellow, yellow lamplight of his humble home play upon his weather-beaten face. It was alive, quickened, moved by the joys of the moment. Both of us relished his reminiscing. An interval of time was being burnished like beaten gold because we were together. Our spirits were warmed and our hearts strangely stirred by the re-telling of his days by the sea.

It did not matter if the clouds outside hung heavy over our heads. What if the overcast was dark and gray? No matter if the snow piled more deeply at the door.

Within that humble little home, and within that hardy old "salt," new, fresh flames of fun and laughter and good cheer were rekindled by my coming.

When we parted, and I picked up my warm winter gloves, he gripped my hands in his great powerful grasp and squeezed them hard. A bright, soft, winsome light shone in his eyes. A wondrous smile of fond appreciation lit up his rugged face.

> The quiet visit had enriched his life and mine.
> The hours spent in gentle interaction were precious.
> Time had been savored, relished and invested with pure joy.

There are scores and scores of solitary, lonely, sad souls in every community. Drawing near to them, cheering them, loving them, caring about them can become pure pleasure.

There can be no finer use of our time.

That really is what the Master meant when He said:

"I was hungry—hungry for human companionship—human warmth—good cheer—and you gave me meat."

"I was thirsty—thirsty for loving care, for a bit of your time—and you gave me to drink."

"I was a stranger—a stranger to the winsome warmth of a genial family—and you took me into your life!"

"I was naked—naked and exposed and vulnerable in a society that strips a man of feeling 'he belongs,' but you clothed me in compassion and tender concern."

"I was sick—sick in soul, sick in spirit, yes, sometimes sick in body—but you cared enough to visit me."

"I was in prison—the prison of my own loneliness, my own fears, my awful sense of being forgotten—*then you came.*" Came to set me free from bondage to my own loneliness.

Yes, yes, yes, we are surrounded by all sorts of men and women who live their little lives in quiet desperation and deep despair. Who long with profound pathos for the warm touch and gentle words of another human who cares. Who wait, sometimes for days, yes even weeks, for the sound of our footsteps at the door; for the calm reassurance of a hearty hug; for the uplift and joy of a joyous joke and lovely laughter; for the strength of our soul to spill out to them.

It costs nothing but time, our time, my time, spent wisely and well, to make this world a brighter, better place. Too many of us look for some polished program or highly organized community scheme to improve the social scene. When all the time at our disposal slips swiftly through our empty hands—unused, wasted, squandered.

Not that this means one must rush about feverishly trying to be a "do-gooder." But it does mean one must be sensitive to God's Gracious Spirit who beckons us to give our time to those He brings across our paths.

As He does this I must remember Christ Himself resides in them just as much as He does in me. He cares for them just as much as He does for me. He presents me with the chance to serve Him and to serve others in these personal encounters. It is His unique and generous method of touching human beings in a tangible, lovely way. . .

in which I can share first hand with quiet contentment and gentle strength.

This is an adventure. Time given in this manner always returns to us in abundant joy. To lose ourselves in others, even for short periods, is to find a new fascination in life, to discover a divine dimension of eternal worth to our little lives.

There is also another perspective to time that is rare and impressive for the wise. We actually do seem to find more of this precious commodity at our disposal. There is time to reflect; time to visit; time to pray; time to commune silently with our Father; time to read great books; time to enjoy inspiring music; time to take quiet walks; time to help those who need a hand or a merry word of good cheer.

The list could go on and on. There are a thousand interests in the earth to engage our attention, to challenge our intellects, to widen our horizons.

Just last week an enthusiastic neighbor told me with great joy of the classes she is taking in arranging flowers. She just loves learning this skill. She went so far as to say she would enjoy working in a florist shop, preparing beautiful bouquets for those who had no time to do this for themselves. For her, it was a delightful contribution she could make to bring special joy and pleasure to others. So it is!

But, also, it is one of those generous gifts bestowed by our Father to enrich the lives of both the flower arranger and those who receive the gift.

One of the beautiful bonuses attending more free time is that it eliminates the stress and scramble of trying to fit everything into a busy schedule. There really is time to relish the moment, to savor the passing scene, to pause and capture the precious encounter.

Admittedly for many of us this is difficult to do. So few of us have learned the humble art of taking time to embellish our days with enduring delight. We are a society "on the go"—rushing in a frantic fever from one demand to the next. We are conditioned to compress the maximum activity into the minimum timespan. For most moderns stress and strain are the warp and woof of life's tapestry.

Quality of life simply cannot be measured nor even appraised by the busyness of our days or the extent of our experiences. It has only one basic evaluation and that is the depth of its serenity and strength of soul for all of us. That must come from Christ Himself.

Allow me to give a simple illustration. Take the appreciation and enjoyment of fine art. It can be lovely drawings, superb photographs, handsome paintings, fine music, stirring poetry, great literature, excellent home crafts, exciting architecture, superior mechanical design—on and on. How much time do I actually devote to an upwelling stream of gratitude within for the river of pleasure and inspiration that flows to my soul from this source?

Do I pause to reflect on the great gift bestowed on the craftsman by Our Father? Do I give thanks for the years of training, discipline and practice invested by the artist? Am I even remotely aware of the sacrifices, the pain, the labor, the thought given gladly to produce such a rare piece? Do I take the time to give it my undivided attention, to salute it with admiration? Do I allow it to enrich me and others with whom I share it?

Just two days ago my attention was suddenly riveted by an unusual painting of an infant asleep on a huge bed.

To one side of him was his much hugged teddy bear. On the other a wild tumble of other toys. It was a work of superb art executed with remarkable authenticity. It was not just a cute, cuddly baby picture. Here was a gifted artist who took you by the hand, with finger over pressed lips, and led you gently to the child's bedside to share a moment of utter serenity.

Again and again I returned to the picture. I was simply lost in wonder, awe and admiration. Here in a single work of art was distilled the very essence of life itself—a tiny tot utterly serene, totally secure, sound asleep in complete composure and perfect peace. I could not help but share the picture with Ursula. She too was enriched, uplifted, held spellbound by its beauty.

All this takes time. It takes thought. It takes my attention. But it is time well invested, bountifully rewarded, leaving an enduring memory of great intrinsic value in the vault of my mind.

What has here been said about fine art in one form or another applies equally in a dozen different areas of our lives. It may be the grandeur and glory of our Father's natural world around us. Christ told us very deliberately to look at lilies, at trees, at birds, at grass, at the splendor of the skies. It may be the gentle smile, the kind features, the bright sparkle in the eyes of a friend or neighbor. Perhaps it is in the unalloyed loyalty of our pets, those charming creatures of great good will, that share our homes and capture our hearts. All of them deserve our time, our thoughts, our attention. And when we bestow time on them in love, we are richer for it. So are they!

It takes time to be holy and wholesome. But it is time well invested for eternity!

2

GENTLE PACE FOR JOYOUS DAYS

"Haraka, Haraka, Hana Baraka!"
Haste, Haste, with no Blessing

It is a very ancient, revered saying in the traditions of East Africa. It was first quoted to me by a silver-haired old man who served as head foreman for the large retinue of laborers who served my father. The old man was Omone. He was short and stocky, suited to his short name. In his rather ungainly little body with its crooked little legs, strong sinewy arms and deeply lined face he bore the heart of a lion wrapped up in the gentle, warm spirit of a saint.

He had the remarkable capacity to get his crews of workers to accomplish more work in a week than most managers achieved in a month. Because Dad preferred to let his employees work by piecework, Omone generally had the day's work done by about 2 o'clock. Then his laughing, singing laborers would hoist their tools over their shoulders and head for home to work their own land.

As a gangling, growing lad in his late teens I always marveled at Omone's achievements. So many employers had endless disputes and half-hearted work from their workers. But around our home there was always this air of good cheer, light hearted humor, and a will to do good work.

Omone insisted the secret was *"Haraka, Haraka, Hana Baraka!"* He simply refused to crowd, pressure or threaten those in his care. He would not push them into a hectic pace where tempers flared or resentment boiled beneath the surface. Instead, he set a steady pace that was both attainable and enjoyable. The result was that people loved to work with him.

It took me a very long time to learn this lovely lesson in my own life, by virtue of the natural instincts inherited from my forebears. Our tradition was to be tough, hard driving, fastpaced people. The main aim was "to get the job done." And, more often than not, to get it done in the shortest time possible. The end result was push, push, push. So doing built up pressure, exerted severe stress on body, soul, and spirit . . . also causing us to forfeit whatever joy there might have been in the job or task at hand.

For years and years of my younger and middle life I missed the pure pleasure of pacing myself to enjoy the activity that engaged my time. The consequence was that I drove myself very hard and often propelled those around me almost to despair. Many friends could not keep pace and grew weary of my own tough impatience.

Looking back in retrospect I now see clearly that my own fast pace of life; my haste in the heat of getting things done; my drive to "go, go, go" or "do, do, do" had combined to turn me into a hard person. Hard on myself, hard on others, hard for God my Father to handle.

But beyond all of this, three other subtle and very adverse attitudes impacted my soul, sealing it off from the gentle grace of Christ. *First,* I found I became very impatient with other people. *Second,* this expressed itself in a short temper that was often critical of my fellows. *Third,* I was less than merciful and fair with my associates.

In actual fact though I seemed to be gaining ground—gaining the whole world around me if you will—I was at the same time losing my own soul.

In my more solemn moments I reflected on this with remorse. Quite obviously I was not a merciful man. The mercy shown to me in such generous measure by God my Father was not passed on to those around me.

The other tired travelers who tramped out their own tough trails seldom received much care, much compassion, much concern, or much mercy from this fast-paced man in such a hurry. And yet, and yet, strange as it may sound the Master stated emphatically several times, *"Learn what it means—I will have mercy, and not sacrifice"* (Matthew 9:13; 12:7).

Like so many of my contemporaries I was too busy;
too preoccupied;
too much in a hurry;
too much on the "go";
too eager to get done!!
To have mercy for others on the way.

"Haste, haste, no blessing"—to either men, God or myself.

On and on I rushed—pushing, pushing, pushing—
Not knowing how to pace myself—my work—my days.
   Then it happened. A most serious illness came upon
me—in part, no doubt, because of my tense, stress-filled
lifestyle. It not only shriveled my soul but also broke my
body. And for months and months I hovered on the brink
of extinction. The doctors gave me less than six months to
live. No medical aid could cure my condition.

Only one alternative remained.
The remedy would be radical!

   Slow down! Adjust the pace of life to the feeble frailty
of diminished strength. Learn to relish the moment. Drink
deeply from the refreshing life spring of Christ's presence.
Take time to be whole and wholesome. Look with compassion and mercy on those around me. Make time to
come to those who suffer, just as Christ comes to me.
Love others, this is the supreme good in life—its main
purpose. Be gentle! These were the lessons I learned—and
discovered the truth of that marvelous Chinese proverb,
"He who travels gently—travels far!"
   At that point in life, I was only 34. It seemed there
really was nowhere to go; no future; no more than an
early grave. Alone, out in the wide expanses of the African
bush, my companions were my beloved Masai people who
had roamed these lion-colored plains for centuries.
   It was they who would come softly to my camps in
the shelter of the spreading acacias. There they would sit
gently in the shade and share their time, their life, their
love with me. First hand they taught me the gentle art of
taking time to reflect; taking time to rest; taking time to
relish the moment.

We sat quietly beside the water holes where they brought their thirsty herds to drink. We conversed quietly about their cattle, their sheep, there grazing, their families, their future as a nomadic race, their response to the love and care of our heavenly Father.

They assured and reassured me again and again that my strength would be restored. They laid their hands on my sunbrowned arms in caring compassion, in a gesture of gentle goodwill, letting me know that my weakened body would yet accomplish much work in the world. Their eyes sparkled with fresh hope as they looked into my tired face. Together we smiled and laughed and chuckled at the bright prospect of enjoying new adventures in life.

This interlude in company with such sterling souls, so free of pretense, so utterly sincere, strengthened my own soul. It was the beginning of a whole new rebirth for a man on the brink of extinction. Little did I dream in those distant days, on those dusty plains, that my Father would sustain me for another forty years.

A large part of the secret was to live at a gentle pace for joyous days!

In essence what I learned was the bedrock veracity of that eternal principle stated by Christ Himself so long ago:

"Take, therefore, no thought for the morrow:
for the morrow shall take thought for the things of itself.
Sufficient unto the day is the evil thereof."

Matthew 6:34

Putting this concept in the simple language of a layman, what He said was: "Simply do not borrow sorrow from tomorrow—do not drag tomorrow's trouble into today."

But most of us do!
We fret and fume and fuss about the unknown future.
We drag tomorrow's imagined difficulties into this day.
So we desecrate each day with stress and strain.
Our Father never intended us to live that way.

He gives us life one day at a time.
   Yesterday is gone.
      Tomorrow may never come.
         Only today is mine to relish at a gentle pace.

It is too precious to overload.
   So it is to be enjoyed in serenity and strength.
      Put first things first.
         The petty distractions can wait.
         Time erases most of them.

Intense research has shown that roughly eighty percent (80%) of all the fears and forebodings we entertain for the future simply never happen. Circumstances change, people change, times change, so all is in flux and our fears are unfounded.

If instead our calm confidence is in Christ, if our quiet faith reposes in our Father, there comes rest to relish this day. He does not disappoint us because He does not change. What is more He alone knows all about tomorrow. So I rejoice in Him. *All is well!*

I sometimes refer to this principle as: *Learning to live in "day tight" intervals of time.* It takes a deliberate, disciplined action of the will to do this. For all around us scores of other voices cry out to us aloud. "Plan your future." "Invest for tomorrow." "Establish your retirement security." "Build a hedge against the unknown," etc.

But a person's life does not consist in what he or she owns. The quality of my life is measured in how my days are relished and enjoyed in company with Christ.

What is accomplished for Him and for others?
What enduring act of eternal value is done this day?
What eternal attitude of love has enriched these hours?

If deliberately, sincerely, I seek Christ's company at the outset of the day, He will clearly direct me how to spend it in joyous good will with Him.

He does not always ask that it be some sort of spiritual endeavor (as we call it). It may be some very ordinary duty as simple as digging a garden; doing the dishes; or even paying some pesky bills. But because He shares all of my life with me, everything He touches through me can become sacred, special and strong.

As a mature man I have learned not to rush things.
There is a great wisdom in steady, serene action.
Most of our mistakes are made in haste!
Many regrets arise out of our rush.

Haraka, Haraka, Hana Baraka

Again and again I have noticed God is not in a hurry. He moves sedately, strongly, surely, serenely through time. If He indeed shares life with me in daily interaction, then I too should be able to enjoy this precious interlude in strength of soul and serenity of spirit. It is precious because He is present to share the day with me!

This is an exceedingly important point which escapes most of us. Too often our main aim is "finish the job" . . . "get things done" . . . "close the deal" . . . "move on to the next activity." They are part and parcel of our pressure cooker way of life. We are so intent on achieving our aims that few of us enjoy the time or effort expended to reach them.

We have not learned the humble art of moving softly through life, taking the time to relish the moment. The surprising truth is that the person who pauses long enough to refresh his soul along the way actually becomes more alert, more alive, more efficient. Life itself is stimulated, energized by an acute sense of our Father's presence on the path with us.

It has taken a long lifetime for me to learn this simple secret. Again and again during the day I turn away deliberately from the demands of my duties to reflect quietly on the ordinary objects which adorn the day. They are gifts from my Father's generous hands. Do I ignore them in my haste, or will I relish them along the way?

Yesterday was a case in point. A tradesman from town came to install new blinds in the living room. It was a tense, stressful task. Several times I slipped outside to walk quietly in the wild garden I love so much. A pair of brilliant, yellow, wild canaries were there foraging for seeds. I was delighted to see them. Their visit made the whole morning brighter and more beautiful. What if the blinds did not quite come up to expectations? What if they did not exactly fit? What if the job was botched?

In spite of all that, it was a beautiful day! For I had found a pair of feathered friends who brought great joy and deep delight into the morning hours.

3

ACCEPTING ALL
AWKWARD PEOPLE

Most of us reach a point in life at which we are aware that much of our stress in soul comes because of awkward people. It will be noticed that I did not say *bad people* or *evil people*, but rather *awkward people*—Those individuals, who, for one reason or another are distinctly different from us and therefore appear to be difficult to accept.

The differences which lie between human beings are so numerous, so diverse, so profound it would take pages and pages to list them all here. But let me name just a handful that seem to produce the greatest problems for people. Certainly these are the ones which alienate our spirits and often tear apart the fabric of our society.

Distinct racial origin—black, white, brown, yellow, etc.

Differences of cultural traditions.

Powerful political philosophies that are opposed to one another.

Intellectual levels of learning that vary.

Rich and poor—the "haves" and the "have nots."

Spiritually minded versus materialistically minded.

The polite and cordial and those who are crude and rude.

Those who are selfish and those who serve others gladly.

The list could go on and on.

But the basic fact which confronts us is simply that we are not all the same. We have different beginnings, backgrounds, upbringings, habits, outlooks on life, aims and aspirations, convictions, characters, conduct, and conversation.

Because of this variation we often perceive other people to be difficult, distinct or at least awkward. We are not always able to accept them as they are. Often we are suspicious, fearful, or even resentful of them.

To protect ourselves we resort to various strategies. We will withdraw from them completely, or keep them at arm's length. If it is within our power, we will try to keep them "in their place." This is commonly called discrimination. We may even go so far as to suppress or subdue them with force, either collectively or individually. This is an attempt to contain them. The end results are often confrontation and outright conflict.

The above does not just apply to the terrible suffering we have witnessed in this century between the Germans and the Jews in Europe or the Whites and Blacks in South Africa. It is what happens in our individual lives between us and our neighbors; between me and my business associates; between me and any other apparently awkward person who crosses my path or enters my life.

It is why Jesus, the Christ, when challenged as to what was most important in all of life, insisted that first and foremost was to love God Himself and next to that to love our neighbors—even if they are atrociously awkward.

But most of us don't do this.
We do not know how to accept God or man.
There is no idea of how to even begin.
That is why I have written this chapter.

Nor did I know how until I learned the hard way. Let me share first a bit of my own background. Then I will paint a word picture of the pain and pathos that I had to pass through in order to accept awkward people. It may well bring great strength to your soul and new hope to your spirit.

As a small lad I grew up as the only white child amongst hundreds of black youngsters living in their thatched huts all around our home. My only playmates were African children who were swift as gazelles, agile as leopards.

They could out-run me, out-climb me, out-throw me in almost any contest. Very quickly I discovered we were very different, very distinct and I was the odd one out.

At a rather early age I was sent off to boarding schools, where, because of my American heritage, I was not always accepted. Especially in high school the British boys found great fun in beating up on me simply because I was a "Yank." Only furious fights seemed to settle the score.

Later in life it horrified me to see how Europeans abused Africans—how Indians from India exploited the primitive people in their employ. And of course, as my travels took me all over the world, I encountered intense and angry discrimination almost everywhere. It was in fact a problem not only of distinct nations, races, cultures or philosophies getting along together, but also, even more importantly, of individual human beings accepting each other.

I gave a great deal of time and thought to all of this. It seemed to me utter hypocrisy to have people always braying about "peace on earth"; "the brotherhood of man" or "'equality for all" when most of us seem unable even to accept the awkward neighbors next door.

Pious platitudes are not the answer.

Nor is it possible to legislate love for one another.

Somehow what is needed is a new view of others.

This was a tough, wrenching, long lesson for me to learn.

One could not enjoy life with constant confrontations.

If there was to be strength of soul and serenity of spirit a man must accept awkward people.

But how?

How does one learn to love an awkward person, without play acting, pretense or being downright phony?

Is there a way to win their affection and allegiance?

My first hard-fisted lesson came with the first ranch I owned as a young man 27 years old. I had been warned well in advance that my closest neighbor just across the road was a difficult, tough, frontier type. He was very much a "loner," who, with sheer determination, muscles of steel and a shrewd mind had hewed out a home for himself in the bush. He lived in a rough log cabin built with his own hands. He even forged some of his own tools out of scraps of steel. He did not welcome intruders and he viewed all outsiders with intense suspicion and distrust.

Our first contact was through his cattle. They were constantly breaking through the flimsy fences and coming to graze on my land. Again and again I took them back to him without anger or recrimination. Instead I used the few moments we met to have a chat, and to ask what his latest project was. Little by little I discovered his greatest passion in life was to repair and rebuild worn-out engines.

Not long after this my tractor broke down. Not being a mechanical man I decided to go over and ask him if he could possibly put it right. I was not at all sure how he would react to my unexpected intrusion. I was hesitant and unsure of myself.

His response was electrifying. Swiftly he gathered up a box of wrenches, screw drivers and other tools and grunted, "Let's go!" To my astonishment he labored until late into the night to repair the tractor. Finally about midnight it roared into life and ran smoothly at full power.

For the first time I saw his rugged features all smiles.

He came into our humble cottage, smeared with oil and grease, to share a cup of coffee and munch on hot scones.

A bridge of friendship had been built between us. It was fashioned from my respect for him and his own desire to be needed and accepted.

The second stern lesson came about twelve years later. I had purchased a large ranch high up in the rugged mountain terrain. On three sides of my holding was all Indian land. Again I was warned that most of my native neighbors were shiftless souls who spent most of their time "hitting the bottle"—"bumming around town"—or just "busting broncos."

This time the tables were turned and our home to begin with was a couple of tents under trees. Then later we moved into a rough log cabin that took grit and hard work to make livable. One day a couple of truly handsome, strong, alert Indians rode down the trail on their ponies and dismounted at my door. I was busy chinking the walls of the old cabin before winter set in.

In gentle, gracious tones they introduced themselves. One was the chief who lived up the valley just beyond us. The other was our closest neighbor just across the fence. When they saw me restoring the cabin they found great delight in recounting its long history; all of those who had lived in it; and all the traditions of their tribe in the area.

It was the first of many visits. They came to accept me almost as one of their own. We would spend hours regaling each other with tales of bears, deer, geese, coyotes and all things wild. Little by little we came to respect, appreciate, trust and need each other.

Once while I was away, a raging forest fire threatened to burn across my land. At great risk to themselves they went out and cut a fire break that saved the whole place. On another occasion the power people were going to build their line across my land while I was overseas. The Indians, all on their own, went up and faced them fearlessly. They forced the company to withdraw their equipment and await my return.

In truth though worlds apart in culture, we had become brothers!

To this day, some thirty years later, those dear people light up with good cheer every time our paths cross. Yet years ago they appeared awkward and difficult.

In a remarkable manner, across the ensuing years, in places as widely separated as British Columbia to the north and Texas to the south, Indians have whispered quietly in my ears, "You really are one of us."

A rare honor indeed from those once far from me.

So again the question must be asked. "How do we accept awkward people?"

There are several specific secrets.

1) People are not always as they appear to us. The dress, the deportment, the distance they keep are often only an outward facade. Some of the warmest spirits are attired only in dungarees. Some of the sweetest souls own little else than a soiled loincloth. Those once strangers can become the closest of friends.

2) Each person, no matter how lofty or how lowly his station in life, owns a private passion. It may be as basic as finding enough food to survive the next day, or as fanciful as collecting fine china. But by quietly taking the time to find out what they love in life, it is possible to "build a bridge" of love and interest across the gap that separates us.

3) Doing this demonstrates in true reality that I do care about them. For it often takes time, thought, and careful attention to find out what lies beneath the facade. And, surprising as it may seem, what lies there is a fierce sense of one's own self-esteem and inner dignity.

4) Even the most difficult people are at heart in search of some respect. Too often they are despised and

rejected because of their awkward behavior. But beneath that tough exterior resides a soul craving recognition.

If I may do so here, once more, let me say I was one of those people. All through my youth, into early manhood, and even later in life I was considered almost antisocial. Most people looked on me as rough, tough and terribly hard to handle. I was regarded as a misfit.

Few were the folks who ever tried to find out the deep inner passion of my soul to know God, or the intense yearning of my spirit simply to be accepted. But God my Father did. Christ my Friend did. God's Gracious Spirit did. And because of the divine touch I was delivered from my utter despair into a life of abundant delight.

5) In essence this is what each of us simply must see. *God, very God, is as much interested in the other person as He is in me.* Christ, the eternal Savior of the world, seeks that awkward one with enduring compassion and generous grace, *just as He sought me.*

Because of this I have no right to despise or disdain difficult people. I may abhor their actions. But buried beneath their wretched behavior beats a soul whom my Father longs to bring into His family.

6) Christians speak much of "loving God." If we are going to demonstrate that love in a perishing world it can only be in two ways. First by complying quietly with Christ's commands. Secondly by accepting the difficult, awkward people around us in whom He already is at work. We begin to see Him in them, just as my Father sees Christ in me.

7) It is this new perspective on *awkward* people which brings strength to my soul. I do not "see" them as antagonists. I see them as lost ones searching for self-worth in God's care. They may not know this. But I do. And therein lies the great adventure of leading them to meet the Master. He always accepts them. And because He does, so can I!

4

How to See Life's Silver Edge

There is a silver edge to life!
The tapestry of our days is embroidered with
blessings.
All is not dark.
Our part is to search for the silver lining.

But how?

How does one find something to celebrate and cheer
about in the midst of so much chaos and
confusion? Where do we look for hope and help in
the ever-deepening darkness and despair of our decadent
age? Is or are there ways to see some light, some love,
some laughter in a languishing world?

The simple answer is yes, yes, yes!

It calls for a certain degree of self-discipline in which
a deliberate decision is made to look for life's silver edge.

It entails cultivating a close personal communion with Christ Himself on the path of life. It demands a calm, sure faith of quiet repose in our Father's care, whereby fresh hope springs up within the soul.

I propose to deal with each of these three activities separately, in order to simplify the subject. But in truth they are closely intertwined like a tightly braided rope made up of three distinct strands.

But before we begin it needs to be understood that life itself is not always even in its distribution of distress. It is true some people appear to pass their days on earth with remarkable ease and a minimum of discomfort, depending on birth, status in society, geographical location and/or fortunate opportunities. Others in sharp contrast endure suffering, poverty and ceaseless struggle.

Because I have lived, worked and experienced life in all sorts of societies at almost every level, what is here presented applies to all people. These are profound and enduring principles which can inject joy into life.

Many of us "moderns," because of our urban lifestyle, have actually lost touch with the earth's environment. It is shocking to realize, for example, that 80 percent of the people in the U.S.A. actually occupy only 2 percent of its land. This means the masses are cramped and crowded into the congestion of giant cities.

Here in the urban environment, designed, engineered and contrived by human ingenuity, human beings are cut off from the healing benefits of fields, forests, streams and the gentle solace of open space, solitude and stillness.

Instead, the population is crowded into a ghastly world of paved streets, roaring traffic, brick walls and the endless assault of noise and chaos in the community. It is no wonder that people turn to mayhem, crime and violence. It is not just a matter of jobs and pay checks that can keep the population from polluting its own environment or if need be igniting it in flames of destruction. This happens because many cities have in fact become a horrible "hell" for those who congregate there.

Our culture has become crude and very corrupt. It is blatantly reflected in the sordid songs and beastly ballads our people compose. It is expressed in the atrocious art that gives expression to our perversion. It is clearly seen in the grossness of our television programs, the raw lewdness of our literature, the subversion of our social mores.

So it is appropriate to ask, "How does one search for the 'silver edge' to life amid all this mayhem and madness of the modern age?" The answer as indicated earlier is one which does demand a certain degree of self-discipline. It calls for a firm determination, quietly and deliberately, to seek spots where sunshine, open skies, a bit of grass, some stately trees, and bird song can bring solace to the soul.

One of my very first jobs as a young person compelled me to live in a large city on the west coast. The company headquarters were located in the toughest part of town. Endless railroad tracks ran everywhere. Trains shunted and clanged and banged around day and night. A mass of manufacturing industries belched smoke, steam and chemical pollutants into the already overcast cloud cover of fog and smog. I moved in a wretched world of concrete, steel and thundering noise.

At times I wondered if it would destroy my sanity and unhinge my mind. Then one day, purely by chance, I came across a small square of grass, surrounded on three sides by some sturdy trees that somehow survived in the awful atmosphere. Their trunks and branches were black with city grime, but still they bore their leaves bravely and the green canopy was like a touch of God's grace in this man-made "hell hole."

Even more astonishing, a small bed of roses had also been planted there. Wonder of wonders, they too managed to push up their blooms amid the gloom. So precious were they to me I would go over at lunch to eat my sandwiches in that spot. In fond affection I would feel their foliage with my fingertips; caress the softness of their petals; inhale the fragrance of their perfume.

The tiny refuge of grass, trees and roses became the silver edge to my life amidst such sordid surroundings. But it took time, effort, thought and daily discipline to spend some precious moments in that place of peace.

Often, our consolation of soul and uplift of spirit come from the commonplace. It is what Christ meant when He remarked, *"Seek and you will find. Knock and it will be opened to you. Ask and you will receive."*

Not sensational things. But strength of soul in simple things.

We of the western world have been deluded by the idea that to find inspiration of spirit or solace of soul we must engage in something sensational or spectacular. Most of us are captivated by the "big show." It matters not whether it be in show business; in the church; in the political arena; in athletics; in big business; or in our own lives. But "big" is not always beautiful and some of our most cherished memories come from the tiniest encounters . . . if we are ready and willing to see life's silver edge.

Yesterday was a classic case in point.

I had invited a friend to attend a local rodeo which has become quite a notorious exhibition. But he was unable to go. Ursula and his wife were going to have a shopping spree. She, too, was not free to come.

So, after our quiet time of early morning devotions I felt urged to suggest that we should instead take a few hours and go out into a little known valley I love so well, to find some peace and quiet.

On the way we passed through a tiny village where we stopped to mail a parcel. As I strolled in the shade of the trees waiting for Ursula a car pulled up to the curb beside me. Out stepped an elderly lady. She smiled warmly, introduced herself and shook my hand. "You won't remember me. I attended your classes months ago. They made such an impact on my life. You are so courageous for Christ." Then tenderly she took my sun-browned arm and looking full in my face with glowing eyes she remarked, "Never lose heart. Always be brave as you are for God!" Oh, what strength of soul she supplied.

It was the silver edge to a gentle day, all unplanned.

Half an hour later Ursula and I strolled softly in the utter stillness of my beloved highland valley. Rugged peaks all around. The scent of sagebrush in the air. A sparrow's distant call.

Ursula whispered, "What stillness!" Another silver edge!

In a very real sense we have to search, and seek, and thus surprise even ourselves with silver linings. We must make up our minds that in company with Christ, led gently by His Gracious Spirit, we can discover pure serenity and strength of soul even in the difficult situations.

Let me provide a simple example. A complicated electrical device in our home began to malfunction. Various friends, expert in mechanical matters, were kind enough to come over and work on the unit. But it only got worse.

Finally, in desperation, we decided to call in a professional service man, whose charges seemed almost prohibitive. He assured us he would come the next day. We stayed home the entire time, but he never showed up, nor did he call to explain why.

A day or so later, I was ill and in bed, when unknown to me, and without warning, he came to work on the unit. Fortunately just then Ursula came home. In an abrupt and rude manner he told her gruffly that the whole unit would have to be replaced. He set a date to come and do this six days later, at 9:00 A.M.

On the agreed date nine o'clock passed and he did not come. Finally he called to announce that he could not do the work that morning. But he assured us he would be there at 2:00 P.M. Again we waited—and waited. Finally about 3:40 his truck appeared. *But he was not in it.*

In all of this we wondered what silver lining we could find amid all this futility and frustration. I reassured Ursula that if we would just remain calm our Father could send us a silver edge. And He did.

I went out to the truck and was greeted by one of the most joyous young servicemen I have ever met. His face glowed with a kindly expression. He bubbled over with good-will. Most important he was a highly skilled, highly efficient repairman. In minutes he had removed all the faulty equipment. He knew precisely what to do. Within an hour he had replaced the whole unit with a much sturdier mounting and superior equipment.

It worked to perfection!

He checked and double checked every detail.

Best of all he was still all smiles. And so were we! Our Father had sent us a double blessing in this dear young craftsman. He was the silver edge to a difficult and trying time.

I was so glad that amid our frustration we had not given away to our emotions; called up the outfit in anger; and blasted them for their shoddy service.

Searching for the silver linings, more often than not, entails searching our own souls. It calls for checking up on our own composure, our own charity, our own inner attitude toward others. If my outlook is askew with anger; if it is warped with resentment; if it is be clouded with distrust; if it is perverted with impatience, it is not likely I shall ever see the silver edge—because I have been blinded by my own behavior.

This is why the Master suggested to us that if we are ever going to be a help to someone else we must first clear the plank of perverse attitudes out of our own outlook. It is the only way we shall ever see the silver lining that adorns the dark and difficult events of life.

There is a dimension to our days which we as God's children need to cultivate continually—namely that it is He who leads us, even into troublesome times. Too often it is assumed that Christ keeps company with us only when things go smoothly and well. We are not aware that He Himself walks through the valley of the shadow of death with us as well. We often forget that He is with us in the fierce flames of affliction. We sometimes feel sure we have been abandoned in the encounters with our adversaries. But this is not so, for He prepares for our well being amid all our adversity.

In a word, finding our Father present, ready to preserve us, is in fact to find the ultimate silver edge to every experience we encounter. I know of no other single perspective in life which lends so much supreme strength to my soul or joy to my spirit.

This cannot be explained or demonstrated in a paragraph or two of a book. It must be learned hour by hour, year by year in a life of close communion with God our Father and Christ our Friend. It is in sharing life with Him that one finds out first hand just how utterly faithful He is to those who follow in His footsteps.

I have written whole books such as *Wonder 'O the Wind, Sky Edge,* and *Thank You, Father* to declare and demonstrate to our sceptical society that He is totally trustworthy. Not just in a theoretical sort of dissertation, but much more convincingly in a first-hand daily experience of His presence.

It is the capacity, the ability, to actually *look for the hand of God in all the events of life, be they good or evil* that enables us to find the silver edge. This practice puts steel in our souls and ignites a flame of gratitude in our spirits. It even brings well being to our bodies when we discover in living truth that His mercies to us are new, fresh, every morning.

5
Rise to the
Challenge

This morning I climbed a mountain. The ascent began at 5:00 A.M. Only the birds and bears and beaver in the river were astir when I left camp alone. It would have been much, much easier to stir up the embers from last night's campfire, warm up with a hot cup of tea, then just take things easy—nice and easy.

Life is so much like that.
Hard choices.
Tough challenges.
Difficult decisions between discipline and dilly-dallying.

We of the western world have become soft people.
We are sated with self-satisfaction.
We prefer leisure and pleasure over taking the measure of challenge that calls for sacrifice.

I first set eyes on this striking mountain when I made camp here late yesterday. This was new terrain for me. Never before had I explored the untamed, wild river that rumbled a few yards from where I slept. As the embers burned low in the campfire the coyotes called to me from the high open slopes of the mountain. So I went to sleep knowing that before dawn I would be on the high rock ridges that soared to the sky.

Yet the challenge was more than just the mountain.

I had purposely slipped away into the wilderness to find utter stillness, to relish intense solitude, and in so doing to be completely alone with God, my Father. This, too, was a tough challenge in our rowdy, chaotic world.

For reasons not well understood by me, Christ, by His Spirit, has been entrusting me with an enormous concern for our perishing planet. The destructive forces of wickedness and degradation that are tearing apart families, wrecking communities and plunging people into perdition weigh heavily on my spirit and soul. In intense intercession I went to meet God on this mountain.

I make no pretense at understanding the mysterious manner in which our Father calls some of us common people into the excruciating challenge of confronting our crude culture. Nor do I fathom His reasons for finding certain plain people whom He feels can enter into the sufferings of His Son for a perishing world.

What I do know is that as I set out in the dim half-light before dawn my whole being—body, soul and spirit—was consumed with compassion for my generation and for my time. I simply could not staunch the tears that cascaded down my cheeks. I tramped heart-broken, shattered in spirit, through the timber and open grass glades on the lower slopes of the mountain.

I make no claims to understand the power of prayer, nor why God in His Sublime Sovereignty honors those of us who cry to Him in our extremity. But I do know He and only He fully hears and completely comprehends our anguish of soul and spirit. And He has condescended again and again to draw near to my broken heart and contrite spirit.

Perhaps His problem is to find someone willing to be broken and bruised in order that others may be made whole? I do not know. I cannot say.

As I broke out above the trees into the open glory of the alpine meadows my horizons widened. But so, too, did the scope of my view of a world headed for destruction. It seemed strange that God's Spirit would wring from my spirit such an outcry of grief over a world gone wrong amid such sublime surroundings.

Faintly I understood why He met with Abraham on Mt. Moriah; with Moses on Mt. Sinai; with Elijah on Mt. Carmel; with Christ His Son on the Mount of Transfiguration. There is something about the stillness, the solitude, the serenity of the mountain summit with God that transforms men.

Though it was cool and chill at break of day, my body was as a furnace at full heat. In absolute agony my hands were lifted in supplication. It seemed strength flowed from my person in powerful waves of impassioned petitions. "O my Father," I cried aloud, "You are the Lord of all the Majestic Hosts of Heaven, honor Yourself upon the earth!" Only the Spirit of Christ could fully convey my deep, deep distress to Christ who fully intercedes for us.

Then there began to flow over my head and face a gentle, refreshing breath of mountain air. And with its coming there enveloped my whole being the calm, quiet, implicit assurance: "My child—I am here—I have heard you—I am at work in the world—I shall have the last word!"

I continued to climb. Now only the short grasses and alpine flowers coming into full bloom carpeted the lofty glades. There was not a single sign of another human footprint on the mountain. It almost seemed a desecration to plant the soles of my feet on such a serene and sacred spot. Gently I tried to walk only on open shale or bare rock lest I bruise a plant.

The great wild, wide valley stretched out below me like a distant map. The river carved its way through the wilderness in giant bows and twisted turns. It was like the river of life, which, like the river of God's generous grace, flows to us forever in glorious bounty. Yet despite the worst men do, the enduring goodness of our Father's faithful concern flows to fallen men.

I stood alone on the summit of gray granite. "O my God, assure me again of Your greatness in all the earth! Not just in the majesty of this mountain wilderness, but also in the chaos and carnage of our inner cities. In the sordid setting of our schools. In the terrible temptations of our bars and bistros. In the carnage of our culture and our commerce!"

And so the struggle of soul surged on and on. It amazed me that my frame could endure such exertion hour upon hour. *Surely, surely,* I wondered, *could one man on a mountain make a difference? God had done it before. He could do it again!* The thought swept through my spirit with enormous energy just then. *It was not possible for me to fully grasp God's ways in the earth. He did not ask me to understand His purposes. He only asked that I be His faithful follower.*

I turned and started back down the slope. Suddenly the swift, staccato wing beats of a wild dove startled me. It lit in a wind-blasted tree nearby. Then a second dove flew from its newly built nest just a few feet from my face. *Doves nesting in such a remote spot, where I had never even imagined they would be found!* The impulse flashed through my mind, then was quickly answered from within my spirit. *Just as My Spirit, too, resides in places you would never think possible!*

With that word of assurance came a great calm. An incredible, almost palpable peace enfolded me. My soul was soothed with enormous serenity. Strength flowed into my whole being, now so open, so available to the Presence of Christ.

I actually began to sing. My mourning had been turned to praise and jubilation.

Half-way down the mountain, by another route, I heard the soft sound of running water. A crystal clear mountain spring burst from below a shelf of rock. I knelt beside it and drank and drank and drank. Then I splashed its cool waters over my face; over my eyes, scalded by tears; over my hands. Refreshed, restored, rejoicing in heart, I hiked back to camp.

There is a stream, a refreshing river of life that flows to us from the presence of God Himself. Today I drank deeply of it. And I am fully satisfied in spirit, strengthened in soul. All is well.

The reader may well ask, where really lies this challenge for God's called out people in our day? The challenge is in our changing world. It is in our changing culture. It is in the changing church. We are faced with the same ringing confrontation which any earnest follower of Christ must meet.

"Seek ye this day whom ye will serve!"
"Ye cannot serve two masters—choose God or mammon."
"Either you are for Me or against Me."

The call of God has not changed across the centuries. It is still a high calling, a noble command to obey Him, a challenge to part paths with a society headed for hell.

The difficulty in our day is that twentieth century Christianity in our western world, under the subterfuge of *tolerance* and *sensuality* (spuriously called *love*) has tried to come to an agreeable accommodation with our corrupt culture. We are a soft society, much more interested in being comfortable with our contemporaries rather than confronting them in concern. We prefer peace at any price rather than plucking people from their eternal peril. We choose to be popular and pack our churches with half-hearted believers, rather than fling down the gauntlet and cry aloud for Christ's followers to count the high cost of personal sacrifice for our Savior.

Nearly half a century ago A. W. Tozer thundered aloud: "The grosser manifestations of fallen human nature are part of the kingdom of this world. Organized amusements with their emphasis upon shallow pleasure, great empires built upon vicious habits, unrestrained abuse of normal appetites are the artificial world called 'high *society.'* These are all of the world which is flesh, builds upon flesh, and must perish with the flesh. These the Christian must put behind him. In them he must have no part. Against them he must stand quietly, but firmly, without compromise, and without fear!"

Therein lies the challenge to which we rise.

Put in its most simple way, what I am trying to say is that we are to be a people who, amid all the changes and chaos around us, live without fear. Not that we insulate ourselves from the calamity of our collapsing civilization, but rather we stand tall amid the ruin with unflinching faith in our Father. Our strength of soul and serenity of spirit come from a calm and unshakable confidence in Christ. We are assured of the sublime companionship of His Gracious Spirit who by His Word can lead us surely and safely through the chaos and confusion of our contemporary world.

Just yesterday morning, after returning from the remote mountain on which I found renewal and refreshment from God Himself, there came a long distance call from a father shattered by the events in his family. From the world's perspective he is an eminently successful businessman. Yet here he was crushed, bruised, beaten by the tragedy and trauma of his teenagers. In his extremity he had phoned me from more than a thousand miles away, pleading for guidance and direction amid his distress.

It is all part and parcel of a perishing world.

This is but a symptom for a society all askew.

This is the challenge of our broken homes, broken hearts, broken dreams, broken hopes.

Are we just going to mutter, "Tut, tut, too bad, too bad, so sad, so sad," then withdraw from the suffering ones, leaving them to struggle on alone in their sorrow?

No, no, no—this cannot be!

Just as the Master did, when He was here, I too must be prepared to enter wholeheartedly into their anguish. The challenge for us Christians is to bind up the broken hearts.

Yesterday we wept together. We prayed together. We talked quietly together in profound communion. And Christ Himself brought strength to our souls.

The world with its sophisticated sociology, with its pathetic reliance on psychology and psychiatry, with its warped and futile academic wisdom sinks ever deeper into degradation. It claims to have a panacea for man's problems while all the time it plunges people ever deeper into despair.

We who trust in God, our Father, should not be ashamed or embarrassed to declare boldly that there is a better way. That way is found in Christ Himself who is and always will be *the Way* of abundant life of satisfaction and strength. The terrible tragedy of our times is that the majority of Christians only know about this way in theory. They hear about it. They talk about it on rare occasions, when pressed on the point. But they themselves know not the sheer delight and strength of soul that come to those who walk in that way. Or put in other words, those who live in Christ and allow Him to live in them hour by hour.

The challenge to which Christ calls His followers is to live in continuous communion with Himself. It is to actually partake of His presence perpetually. It is to be acutely aware that His life is being imparted, transmitted to me, directly by intimate personal interaction. This is not some sort of flight of fancy or sensational spirituality that eludes most people. It can be the daily habit of anyone who truly desires to know Christ in the power of His resurrection.

If a father, in anguish of spirit, can call me from more than a thousand miles away, and we share each other's life in the most profound pathos and at the deepest levels of human experience—why cannot it happen with Christ who is here? I could not see my friend's tear-stained cheeks. I could not touch his burning body. Yet we were one in spirit, one in soul.

Why then are we daunted by a sceptical society that chides and derides us for claiming to know Christ, to actually share His life? Without seeing Him, without touching Him, I still share His life in joy. He is my strength of soul!

6

DEALING WITH DEATH

In our contemporary world it is common to circumvent the matter of death by attempting to shield ourselves from facing its dark reality. This is especially true in the area of our own personal lives or in the lives of those close to us. It is not a subject we care to discuss openly or face fearlessly.

There is a peculiar paradox in all this. Increasingly we are exposed to the pain and anguish that attend death all over the planet. Almost daily crime, violence, murder, wars and carnage invade our homes, impact our minds and scar our spirits. Yet, more often than not, we only shake our heads in disbelief and behave as though it could only happen to other people in other places. So that in a sense we become scarred in soul shrugging off the specter of death as though it really was a distant tragedy.

Some of us, of course, have been intimately involved with death, not only in our own families, but also among our friends. It is for this reason that I felt constrained, a few years ago, to write the book *Sky Edge*. For if we are going to be people of intellectual integrity and moral certitude we must grasp what death is all about from God's perspective.

From a purely human viewpoint, death spells out only problems of pain and separation and disaster. This is one of the main reasons we do not care to discuss it. Also there attends it a mystery which is beyond most of us to understand with our finite human comprehension. So we prefer to shy away from the subject. We shrug our shoulders and dismiss it with some foreboding.

But as God's children, in His care, we need to clearly understand death if we are to enjoy inner strength of soul. I say this in great earnestness. For death has much more to do with life than most of us ever dream. It does not just consist of terminal illness, fatal accidents, ambulances, funeral services or graveyards. Death is the basis of life itself!

Those last seven words may startle most readers.
They are absolutely true.
Allow me to explain.

When God, our Father, first prepared the planet for human habitation, it was His intention that it should be a perfect paradise. That is to say, because it was "good" from His perspective, it was free of anything which would defile or degrade it. In other words, it was a realm exempt from deterioration or decomposition. It was to be an enduring, eternal environment of sublime serenity and remarkable harmony between God and man. In this setting there was to be no discord, no deception, no decay. In close company with God Himself man would be undefiled, yes, even immortal . . . exempt from death.

But the divine disclosure given to us mortals by God Himself, through His Own Spirit, is that this sublime state of affairs was short-lived. His perfect plan for the planet was short-circuited. Because two profound principles of perversion entered paradise. The first was the dreadful deception of man and woman by God's archenemy, Satan. He declared blatantly, *"You shall not die."* An utter lie! The second principle was the immediate consequence of the initial deception, *"Death entered in—(i.e. followed)."*

The immediate confrontation between "good" and "evil" became known as the "curse," better understood as *"the dominion (domination) of death"* over the entire planet. There is a great mystery to all this, referred to in God's Word as "the mystery of iniquity."

Put in the plainest possible layman's language, it refers to the concept that everything on earth is conditioned by death. Everything is subject to defilement, degradation, decay and, in the end, death and dissolution. Everywhere, all around us, death is under way in a world system set against God who is life and the giver of life.

Even more difficult for most of us to grasp is the profound principle that now exists whereby only through the on-going process of death does life emerge to repeat the cycle.

For example, you the reader only have life at this moment because other life forms have died in order to sustain you. Living grain is cut down, harvested, crushed and milled, then baked into bread to nourish your body. All sorts of fruits and vegetables flourishing in the sun are suddenly plucked, placed on your plate to provide life and sustenance. Fish and fowl, cattle, sheep and other livestock all have their lives cut short. Through their slaughter and death you derive proteins and minerals to support your body structure.

From death comes life!

Only God Himself can deliver us from the carnage.
The cycle of birth—life—death—rebirth goes on.
The scientists call it "The energy conversion cycle"!
Our Father has entered it to give us "a new birth."
Or as we sometimes call it, "a conversion."
This is accomplished by Christ who gives us His life.

So, just as in the natural realm (the physical planet) there is birth—life—death—rebirth. So likewise in the moral and spiritual realm there is birth—life—death—rebirth.

As God's people we need to learn how to deal with death. It is not something distant in the future which people sort of dread, it is a phenomenon, a principle (i.e. the law of sin and death) which surrounds us on every side. It is an integral function of every aspect of our sojourn on the planet. And only Christ can provide abundant new life amid all this death.

We live on a perishing planet.
We live among a perishing people.
We are surrounded by a fragile perishing biota.

We share existence here with all other perishing life forms be they trees, plants, flowers, fish, animals or birds.

And, strange as it may seem, despite all the effort and expertise and work and thought man expends to try to reverse the trend, all he possesses is depreciating. In a phrase drawn from an old hymn, "Death and decay in all around I see!"

Therein lies the great enigma to all of life.
Am I going to spend my life, my energy, my time,
my thought, my skills, my love only on what
perishes?

Do I pursue only those things which pass away?
What is the primary purpose of life?

Surely there must be more to a person's earthly sojourn than to sink down in despair because death is
everywhere.

This is the philosophy of the worldling.
It is the bleak emptiness of those without hope.
This is the ennui and cynicism of those apart
from God.
Their life theme is, *"Eat, drink and be merry—for
tomorrow we die!"*

But for those of us who have found new life in Christ,
who have come to know God as our Father, who are
renewed by His Spirit daily, there is a brand new dimension to life. And our life theme is, *"For me to live is Christ—
for the principle (the law), the power, of the spirit of life in
Christ Jesus (the living Lord) has set me free from the law
of sin and death."*

My whole life is no longer conditioned by death. The
parameters of my earth sojourn are no longer determined
by the spectre of death. I am not just a perishing pessi-
mist, trying to pile up a few paltry possessions which can
do nothing to deter death. Instead I have passed from
death into life—God's life which endures forever.

I have been delivered from despair into the wonder of
His love.

I have been taken out of darkness into the splendor of His light and understanding.

The only possible way in which we can deal with death adequately and properly is through the very life of God. The only perspective which can overcome the despair of death in all of its insidious forms is the liberating love of God. The only sure, shining hope and assurance given to perishing people in a dark world is the wondrous illumination and light of God Himself, who comes to us in Christ.

Allow me to deal with each of these in detail, but also rather briefly.

1) *The Life of God in Christ*

This caliber of life is distinctly divine. It is of the Spirit of God. It far transcends ordinary physical or biological life common to planet earth.

The supreme definition of life is that interaction or interchange between an organism and its environment. The instant an organism is no longer able to derive its sustenance from its surroundings it is declared to be dead. All forms of life on planet earth derive their support from the earth environment. But because it is conditioned and dominated by death these natural life forms at least are only transient and temporary.

On the other hand, God our Father surrounds us by His Spirit, His presence, His supernatural power, and invites us to draw on His eternal, abundant life. As we interact with Him, commune with Him, drink of Him, partake of Him, believe in Him, we experience and are energized by His eternal life.

This is the principle Christ referred to when He declared boldly:

*"It is the Spirit that quickeneth (makes alive):
the flesh (ordinary human life) profiteth nothing."*

This is simply because it does not endure, and at best is very transient. Its tenuous, temporary dimension defrauds us, for it passes away. Whereas the life of God endures forever.

We see the life of God in its clearest colors in Christ. In fact He went so far as to say, *"I am the Way, the Truth, and the Life."* He is the divine demonstration of God's life.

That life overcomes disease and illness.
That life restores deranged minds and twisted emotions.
That life realigns wrong wills with God's good will.

That life redeems sin-wracked souls from self-destruction.
That life transforms sinners into sons of God.
That life recreates human character and conduct.
That life bestows immortality on the human spirit.
That life utterly dispels the specter of death.

So tremendous was the energy of that life in Christ that even when His adversaries crucified Him, His mutilated body did not undergo corruption. Death could not contaminate, defile or destroy His supernatural person. The rock tomb could not restrict or restrain His radiant resurrection. Even all the demonic forces of evil, nor hell itself, could confine the Living Christ. He triumphed over every evil arraigned against Him, because of His divine life.

That is why the ringing, jubilant, irrepressible catch-word of the Church will ever be, *"He is risen—He is alive!"* And I would add again, *"He is here, offering us, as always, His life, if we will receive Him!!"*

2)   *The Love of God*
Is but the demonstration of the life of God. It is our Father, in His boundless generosity and magnanimous grace, giving Himself to any person humble enough to receive Him. He gives Himself to us in a wondrous out-pouring of forgiveness. He gives Himself to us in the lovely friendship of His Son. He gives Himself to us in the gentle guidance of His Spirit. He gives Himself to us in the remarkable, wondrous commitments of His Word. He gives us His precious presence daily.

3)   *The Light of God*
Is all of the foregoing which are found not only in our Father's faithfulness to us, but also in our communion with Christ, our dearest Friend. And in His Gracious Spirit, our beloved Guide, through the darkness and despair of our earth sojourn.

We see clearly because of His illumination that it is only His life which can counteract all the corruption and decadence of death around us. We see it is only His love which can dispel all the despair and degradation of a sin-scarred society. We see, without doubt, that it is the radiant light of Christ Himself, who is *"the light of the world,"* that dispels the darkness to bring us into the joy of His presence.

Just yesterday morning I went to see a tough, pro-fane man about a piece of land he owned. On the way the deep conviction came to me that his soul was much more the reason for my visit than his land.

As we walked over the wild acres, lying warm to the sun, beside a singing mountain stream, he spoke to me in a torrent of profanity. But I was sure beneath his tough hide and sun-burned face there struggled a soul facing death. He was old in years; decrepit in body; worn out with work.

Before I had been there an hour he unburdened his heart; unbuttoned his soul; and with tear-filled eyes told me of the death, devastation and despair that dogged his days.

As we stood together on the sagebrush bench, its rich fragrance filling our nostrils, I spoke to him gently of our Father and His love. I introduced him to Christ our Friend who offers us His life that overcomes death.

He listened intently. He accepted joyously. We prayed together standing out in the open wind blowing off the snow peaks. He was reborn. We had dealt with death. God's life had triumphed. We parted as friends.

7

HOPE FOR
EACH EVENT

Looking at life from a purely human perspective, it seems as if we are in an era of human history in which there is very little hope on the horizon. An ever increasing number of problems face the community of man. In increasing hordes people live in poverty and privation. The discrepancy between rich and poor grows ever wider and deeper. It has been documented in various reports that the top two percent of wealthy Americans possess more wealth than the entire bottom forty percent of its people. There is among the masses a growing sense of hopelessness in the midst of increasing crime, violence, illiteracy, family break-up and growing corruption in our culture.

Compounding all this carnage is the deliberate effort of certain vested interests to dominate society. It is no secret that the ever pervasive appetite and greed for power that is a hallmark of unregenerate human nature will drive men and women to do the most despicable deeds. Using the influence of money, the media and human idealogies various schemes are spawned to manipulate the masses and bring them into subjection to evil ends.

This has always been the saga of human history on this perishing planet. Always, ever, behind the scenes, not even recognized by most men and women, there is at work the mystery of iniquity. The unseen enemy of men's souls, Satan himself, and all his minions of evil spirits attempt to accelerate the demise and destruction of the human race. Through subtle deception and world-wide delusion the multitudes of mankind flounder and fall under the sinister influence of sin and self-preoccupation.

Amid all the darkness and despair Christ comes to us offering us release and freedom from our fears. He comes telling us to be of good courage. He comes bringing us His hope.

This hope and this help is not just "pie in the sky."

The promise of assurance is not just for heaven.

This dimension of good cheer is for here and now.

It is a dimension of delight, optimism and confidence which alone can overcome the chaos and confusion of our culture. It is a capacity imparted to God's child to be tranquil and triumphant in the throes of trouble. It is the ability to possess our souls in hope while all around us there is despair.

This hope is not some sort of wishful thinking. Nor is it to indulge ourselves in self-delusion that "Things will turn out all right in the end." It is not even the power of positive thinking that attempts to put on a bold, brave front in a faltering world.

Our hope is in God our Father.
Our confidence is in the Living Christ.
Our strength is in His Holy Spirit.

Without being drawn into a difficult doctrinal discussion, I shall set out several very simple reasons for saying this. They can be grasped readily by the most ordinary person. Even a child can understand.

God is absolutely supreme and all-powerful in the universe, in all knowledge, and in all His purposes. No other force or energy is equal to Him. Therefore ultimately He always triumphs. He has the last word!

His intentions are always pure, noble and constructive because of His impeccable character and perfect conduct. So His inherent goodness and grace dispel sin and selfishness. His light drives out darkness of any kind. His wondrous love demolishes despair. Because He is here!

It is His presence which brings us poor people peace. It is His power which brings serene strength to our souls. It is His purity which injects great hope into our lives amid a sordid society.

For these reasons a Christian can look at life calmly.
It is possible to live in peace amid great perplexity.
We can find hope in each event.
For He shares it with us.

As ever of old, from the most ancient of times His quiet, strong assurance is, *"Peace be unto you. Be not afraid. It is I!"*

Those of us who relish His companionship find this true. In quietness and confidence our hope is renewed afresh. His profound communion with us—that of Father,

Friend, and Fellow Companion on the path of life—brings serenity, surety and strength to our souls.

The one great flaw in our human conduct which can prevent this from being our exhilarating experience is our tendency to be distracted and dismayed by the events around us. The world is very much with us. We are caught up in the vortex of changing circumstances, changing people, changing pressures.

Our absolute center must be Christ.
Our unshakeable confidence must be in His character.
Our part is to practice and partake of His presence.
"O God, You are here! You are near! You are dear!"
Then all is well. Hope is born anew. Peace prevails.
And we calmly see His commitments carried out for us.

The reader may wonder just how this works out in the stress and struggle of everyday life. Allow me to give an illustration from the past few weeks.

A short time ago a heart-rending phone call came from a woman in dreadful distress. She is stricken with a disease that has crippled her body and confined her to a wheelchair. In tears and anguish of spirit she poured out her awful story. In the midst of this calamity her husband had left her. And others to whom she turned for help only abused her.

The disease which afflicts her is more than a monster that has deformed her body. It wracks her whole being with intense pain. So here is one who not only endures awful physical agony but also emotional anguish.

As if to compound her dilemma, those in the medical profession entrusted with her care were extremely cruel to her.

In her despair she wept and wept.
> Here were circumstances in which there was no hope.
> In her extremity she felt constrained to call me.
> What could I do?

I am not, nor have I ever been, one of those men who tried to impress others with prestige or prominence in society. Nor have I tried to cultivate the company of "important people." I do not have any "special connections" or the inside information to get things done by human agencies.

> I told this dear, desperate woman as much.
> There was no one I could call; no one I could see;
> no one I could prevail upon to help her in her plight.

But I assured her calmly I could call on Christ. I inquired if she would let me pray earnestly on her behalf that our Father would intervene in her dilemma. I quietly told her that He was the sure source of hope in her distress. Amid her tears she agreed to let me intercede with God's Gracious Spirit on her behalf. So in childlike confidence we asked for divine, supernatural help beyond our knowing.

It took only a few moments. Then she became composed.

Yesterday afternoon the phone rang again. It was she. She was utterly ecstatic. In a remarkable way she had suddenly been taken to an excellent care unit. They had given her a lovely private room. She was surrounded with people who gave her loving assistance. Her pain had subsided. She even loved the color of the drapes. Hope sprang anew!

This is the sort of event in which it is God our Father who demonstrates that He Himself is our hope. In the crisis it is Christ who can care for us. It is the sure solace of His Spirit who can bring peace amid pain and perplexity.

What I am pleading for here again is for those of us who follow Christ to focus our attention on God Himself in times of turmoil. Too often we are distracted by the difficulties around us. We are easily overwhelmed by cruel circumstances. We cannot seem to see our Savior, our Sustainer amid the storms of sorrow, suffering and stress.

But He is in the storm with us!

There is a magnificent passage in the little known prophecy of Nahum which I just love, *"The Lord hath His way in the whirlwind and in the storm, and the clouds are the dust of His feet!"* Nahum 1:3

"Yes, O God, You are here!"
"Yes, You are here to help."
"Yes, O Christ, You can deliver!"

Our part is to trust Him calmly. To thank Him in quiet assurance. To wait surely in hope. For He is our hope!

At the close of this century we Christians need to come back to this bedrock of our beliefs. We must return to the basic resources found in God Himself. We are compelled to make a simple choice, "Trust God or trust human technology."

The contemporary church is preoccupied with its high profile preachers; its all pervasive programs; its use of "people power"; its pathetic dependence on pastoral counseling that often relies on psychology and psychiatry.

Christ calls us back to find our hope in Him.

Our Father beckons us back to implicit prayer.

His Gracious Spirit gives generously of His faith that we might trust God as little children do.

I have introduced the exercise of faith in our Father at this point on purpose. For hope is bound up with faith. They cannot be separated. Faith, hope and love in Christ are the three essential ingredients which, when combined together, form the concrete mix of Christian experience, just as cement, sand and water when combined in the construction industry produce concrete.

Without basic, childlike confidence in Christ we are weak-kneed people easily perplexed by our pressure-cooker society. Changing circumstances and adverse events dismay us. But with unshakeable assurance that our Father is arranging our affairs we become formidable people of faith. Our hope is in Him!

Beyond this we must learn to believe assuredly that Christ is capable of making every experience turn out for our final good. We may often have to wait a long time to see this happen. In some cases years will pass before we fully understand the reason for our pain or tears.

This is one of the rich benefits that come to us as we wait on God. From year to year bountiful bonuses are bestowed on us as we watch with wide-eyed wonder the ways in which our Father brings great good out of our difficult days. But in faith and confidence we must learn to look for His hand at work in the details of our little lives—then give hearty thanks for His help and hope bestowed upon us.

Then, too, it is essential for us to be convinced in soul and spirit that when we ask Him to lead us aright,

He does! So often when events appear to go wrong; when the way becomes difficult; when disaster seems to overtake us our faith fails. We even feel forsaken.

But His assurance to us is that He does not forsake us. He is here to sustain and deliver. Therein lies strength of soul!

Intermingled with faith and hope there is that third essential ingredient—*Love, the remarkable concern and care of God for His children.* I am not speaking here of the spurious, sentimental love which is bandied about so much by our contemporary society. I am referring to the incredible, amazing, splendid, self-giving love shown by God to men.

Apart from that divine love we would all perish.

It is the elemental source of all creative energy in the cosmos.

That supernatural love overcomes all evil.

It is the supreme good that prevails over all that is evil.

Because our Father pours out this love in His life for the planet we as a race are preserved from utter destruction. It is this bedrock of belief that enables the Christian to face every event with faith and with hope. For Christ the Lord God really is there to care for us in His love.

We dare not allow the turmoil of the testing time to distract our attention from His presence. No matter how devastating the crisis of cruel circumstances may seem to us, we must come back to Him amid the mayhem. Again, and again, and again I cry out to Him verbally, audibly, vehemently, "O Living Christ, You are here because You care! You, and You alone, can deliver me, sustain me, assure me in this hour!"

Bless His dear name, He does!
In the crisis He brings calm.
In the storm He bestows strength.
In the alarm He brings love.

So it is that love, faith and hope spring up afresh. I am renewed, preserved and made whole.

Out of overwhelming gratitude I in turn then love Him; follow Him in quiet faith; rejoice in the bright hope that rises up within my soul and spirit. All because of Him.

"Oh my soul, hope thou in God!"

Psalm 42:5 & 11

8

THE GLORY
OF GRATITUDE

Gratitude is the grease of good will which lubricates the machinery of our day-to-day, person-to-person, man-to-God actions. We have the simple choice either to grind and grumble our way through life finding fault, or to bubble over with gratitude and thanks to God and man.

Gratitude is not some mystical gift bestowed upon us by the abundant Spirit of the Most High. It is not a personality trait inherited from my parents. Nor it is some sort of delightful disposition put on to charm others.

Genuine gratitude is a deliberate action of my will that determines daily to express hearty thanks for all that comes my way, no matter what it is. In the simple, straightforward language of Scripture it is this, *"In everything give thanks!"*

To do this in sincerity and good-will is challenging. It far surpasses play acting or false pretense. It is much more than putting on a brave front when beneath the surface my spirit is sour and my blood is boiling. Most of my contemporaries and God, my Father, can tell whether or not my gratitude is genuine.

Spontaneous, joyous gratitude really is the *elixir of life.*

There is nothing else which produces so much contentment.

The attitude of gratitude really makes us glow.

The reason for this is hidden from most of us. We wonder why thoughtfulness transforms us. There really is a secret to the glory that engulfs us.

It is this: instead of being preoccupied with our own problems, pain, protests over every petty complaint, we look out beyond ourselves to the goodness of God and others. Instead of seeing life through the narrow slot of our own self-centeredness we take the wider view of realizing all we have, all we are, all we enjoy, comes to us freely, generously from our Father's gracious heart and open hands.

As I pen these lines, it is early morning, and in the gray dawn a steady, heavy rain is pounding on the red tiles of our roof. The water is flowing strongly in the eavestroughs. It is gushing down the drainpipes, running over the hill, spilling into the great, gray basin of the lake below us. It has rained all night, which is unusual in this hot, dry, semi-arid northern desert. It appears it may rain all day. . . all weekend!

There are a number of reasons one could complain about the unexpected storm. All the day's plans to clean up the yard will have to be deferred. The neighbors keep insisting the rains stimulate so much weed growth no one can keep up. All the picnics planned have to be put off. The heavy rain will split the cherries and ruin the crop. Campers will have to fold their soggy tents and head for home. No warm sun to enjoy on the beach, only gray skies, dark clouds, wet, wet!

By contrast we can see the rain as a special gift from our Father's loving hands. Already it has quenched scores of forest fires that had previously scorched the earth and hills. Its generous flow is refilling the springs and streams and diminishing reservoirs. It clears the atmosphere charged with smoke and dust from weeks of drought. It removes the heavy pollution of pollen that makes allergies so common. It refreshes the whole earth in glorious ways that no human technology could match. It really is a beautiful bounty!

In hearty appreciation I went to stand at the great wide windows. With upwelling gratitude I gave thanks again and again. From deep within my soul there arose, not a complaint, but a joyous acceptance of this precious gift bestowed in such abundance. My Father does care— He does know what is best. Instead of finding fault with the heavy rain, a gentle glory enfolds my world.

I have a very special friend, an elderly octogenarian, who came into my life only a few years ago. The one aspect of his character which draws me to him, more than any other, is his joyous gratitude for all that befalls him. Despite fragile health; despite the adversities of old age; despite diminishing strength every time we meet he is bubbling over with gratitude to God for every experience that comes his way.

It is pure pleasure to be in his company.
His eyes still sparkle with mirth.
His mind is sharp with thanks.
His conversation is laced with laughter, praise
and gratitude for all of God's good gifts.

Because of his buoyant spirit and bright outlook one comes away filled with good cheer, contented in heart.

It is of special interest to know and understand how this optimistic outlook came about in his life. Recounting it here briefly may help to reshape our own souls.

Up until very late in life his one consuming passion had been his business interests. He was a wholesale distributor for a large firm on the coast. Sales, sales, sales were the sum total of his life, his time, his strength.

Then one day a few years ago he was high on a ladder cleaning windows on his handsome home when the ladder slipped. He crashed from the top, falling down fourteen concrete steps into a yawning stairwell that led to the basement below.

He was sure his end had come.

And in the crisis his spirit swept over his life in swift retrospect. What had he lived for? What had been first in his affairs? If spared, what would he do with the rest of his days?

Then and there, broken and bleeding, he decided to give God thanks and genuine praise, no matter what. And, as by a miracle, he did recover!

True to his commitments to Christ, he has never deviated from his determination to give genuine thanks in all things. The end result is that he has touched hundreds of lives for the Master. He has brought enormous benefits to his family. He has warmed and enriched the hearts of his friends.

It takes time to give thanks.
It takes thought to give thanks.
It takes tenderness to give thanks.

It matters not whether our appreciation is expressed to God our Father; to our families; or to others around us. The very act of doing so may require writing a warm-hearted letter of appreciation. It may involve making a special phone call. Or it may even demand a personal visit to express the depth of genuine gratitude felt within.

It is also very rewarding to give careful thought just how best to show one's appreciation. It means so much to the recipient when stated in honesty and sincerity without sham or flattery.

Finally, gratitude can be a glorious element in life when it is expressed in tenderness. Too often it is given in an off-handed manner, almost as though it really was of no consequence. Quite the reverse is true. When spoken in tenderness and earnestness it can become an enduring benediction, a gesture of good will that builds enduring bonds of affection.

A small and yet very precious incident that happened several years ago will illustrate what I am trying to say. I had gone to the home of a young minister to encourage him and his wife in their work. They lived in a very tough community. So, as is often my custom, I called around to cheer them up and to strengthen their faith in Christ.

It was getting dark outdoors. Through the dusk I climbed up a narrow path to reach my car parked up on the road above. In the dim light I could see a young woman standing at the top of the trail. As I approached closer I greeted her, though I did not recognize her at once.

After we exchanged a few pleasantries, she suddenly remarked: "Are you Mr. Keller?" I affirmed that I was. Then suddenly she did something very unusual.

"You are the man who introduced both my mother and my dad to Christ years ago. He has transformed all of our home, our lives, our whole family!" It was an outburst of pure appreciation expressed with remarkable sincerity. For I had not seen the family for years.

Swiftly, warmly, she flung her arms around me in a gentle but genuine bear-hug. "Thank you! Thank you!" she repeated softly for several moments.

As I drove home, the memories of the day I had dealt with her parents flooded over me in crystal clarity. When she was just a tiny tot, her mother had been placed in a special medical care unit where the prognosis was hopeless. Her dad was desperate, far from God, and in deep despair.

But Christ had come and changed all of that! What hope, what help, what joy and happiness He bestowed.

And in the twilight of that night the daughter had shown such superb gratitude.

That is the sort of action that brings sudden glory into the most ordinary day. She was not ashamed to show her genuine gratitude. Because of it not only had she enriched my life, but she had also brought great joy to our Father's heart of love.

This, as I understand it, is true praise to God and strength for our own souls.

I state this in utter sincerity. We, as ordinary men

and women on the rocky road of life, need to know we are appreciated. We need to hear those simple yet stirring words that strengthen our souls, *"Thank you!"* We need the inspiration of spirit that comes to us when someone cares enough to stop and say, *"Well done!"* This is all part of the profound pleasure in living which gives purpose to our pilgrimage and direction to our days. It quickens our step, puts a smile in our eyes, then sets us to singing.

And in exactly the same manner God, our Father, needs our gratitude. Again and again I have heard speakers remark, "God has everything at His disposal. He does not need us!" That simply is not true. It is a lie! He made us for Himself. He yearns over us as His beloved children. He draws us to Himself. He longs for our sincere love and cooperation. He delights in our genuine gratitude and thankfulness. We can bestow no greater honor upon Him than to express our profound appreciation. It brings Him joy and blessing beyond our understanding.

Hundreds of times in His Word He encourages us to actually bless Him, to honor Him, to praise Him. Not in some stilted, sanctimonious manner that is organized or arranged by a structured church service. But rather in the sincere, spontaneous, often very private outpouring of our souls to Him in intimate communion.

It takes time. It takes thought. It takes tenderness to express this genuine gratitude to God, as well as to man. It means getting alone with Christ as my closest Companion and dearest Friend. It involves an audible, heart-felt outpouring of wonder, awe, and adoration to my Father. It calls for quiet, still, inner communion of my spirit with His Spirit.

I must get alone with God to adequately express my gratitude to Him.

Christ Himself did this when He lived on earth.
  His choicest people have done it all down through history.
  He calls us to do it today to strengthen our souls.

Each of us must find our own private trysting place with Him. There has to be a special rendezvous. It will become not only our precious place of peace, but also our hour of strength and serenity.

Some will find it in their so-called "closet" where they close the door to outside distractions. Others may find it in their garden; a quiet corner of the home; in the still sanctuary of an empty church; out on a quiet walk; or just tucked away in some solitary spot in the woods, by the sea, in a park, or on a mountain.

The latter has been best for me—away from the cramped confusion of our crowded and chaotic world. These interludes should not be programmed. They must never degenerate into mere ritual or routine. They need to be spontaneous, shot through with up-welling thankfulness, charged with joyous gratitude. The entire impetus originates with the generosity of God; the greatness of God; the goodness of God; the grace of God; the grandeur of God; the gentleness of God.

Not just in a spiritual dimension—but also in the very precious impact of His presence in all of life around us.

I sense and see Him in the earth, the fields, the forests.

I sense and see Him in the flowers, grass and shrubs.

In singing streams, in whispering pines, in a thousand bird songs His presence, His peace, His power comes to me and I give thanks.

I recall His healing of all my diseases; His restoration of my soul; His uplift of my spirit. Then gratitude floods from within.

I give thanks aloud for all His benefits of wisdom and strength: For friends and fellow believers; for His faithfulness always, always!

Amid all this thanksgiving He is blessed, and my own soul is made strong in Him.

9

HUMOR THAT
HELPS AND HEALS

There is humor; and there is "humor"! There is light-hearted hilarity; and there is "black humor," as it is called by those dealing with crime.

There is wholesome fun; and there is dark cynicism.

There are clean jokes; and there are gross stories with a double meaning suggesting illicit sex.

There is good cheer; and there is cruel sarcasm.

The list could go on and on. We as God's children need to know the difference. There is a joyous humor which comes to us as a beautiful benefit from our Father. It brings help in the hard places. It bestows healing on broken bodies, broken hearts and broken hopes. I consider it one of the choicest gifts bestowed upon the human race for our well-being and contentment.

But, by the same measure, there is abroad in our society a sordid cynicism spawned by those who do not know God our Father. In their despair and in their darkness they devise a cruel sarcasm which belittles that which is noble, and demeans all that is beautiful. This snide humor proliferates all around us. It is common in our books, journals, newspapers and the most popular T.V. programs. It is promoted as something sharp and sophisticated, yes, even very clever. And to my surprise, some Christians actually enjoy it.

We find this sort of jesting and degrading humor used frequently by preachers, speakers and teachers to win popular acclaim. One of the largest churches on the continent is packed full of people—because the pastor is "so very funny." When asked what he taught them from God's Word, none of those interviewed seemed to remember much. But always, always, they could recount his jokes with the added comment, "This man is an absolute blast! His humor just blows you away!" And so the church becomes a circus.

It is with an acute anguish of spirit that I recall a personal encounter of this sort just over 30 years ago. I was at the critical point in my search to truly know Christ. Some friends urged me to attend a special conference where a high profile speaker from the southern states was the star attraction. Every one of his lectures was laced through and through with funny stories, off-beat wit and suggestive humor. Most of his gullible audience thought he was hilarious. But I was utterly dismayed. In fact I felt betrayed and deprived of the eternal truth for which my soul hungered so desperately. I was angry enough to let him know. Whether or not it ever changed his clowning around was never disclosed.

In bold contrast to this sort of conduct, there is a calibre of good cheer, high humor, and wholesome fun which can enrich all of life. Not just for ourselves but also for the joyous well-being of others around us. All my friends know full well how much I enjoy a hearty joke. They often comment about the contagious mirth and deeply genuine joy and laughter that erupts from my soul. They love to hear me chuckle. They relish the light-hearted stories I recount, many of which reveal how high humor and good cheer are an important part of the bright tapestry of our days enriched by God.

I am not ashamed of this side of my makeup. For it is a wholesome antidote to all the sorrow, stress and sin of our tragic times. Very often the capacity to "to see the funny side" of a difficult dilemma brings balance and composure into the crisis. This high humor can often defuse stress and diminish anxiety or anger. This is a vital part of life if we are to be people who are slow to anger and merciful in spirit.

Shortly after the incident related above, about the high profile preacher and his peculiar puns, I was invited to spend some time on a mission boat that served Canada's Pacific Coast. On board were crusty old salts whose lives outflowed with humor.

They were engaged in very dangerous duties, shepherding a small ship through the powerful storms and perilous waters of "The Graveyard of the Pacific"! More than that they came with good cheer to all sorts of crusty characters who made the remote reaches of the wild and rugged West Coast their home.

They ministered with heart-felt compassion co-mingled with hearty humor to loggers, fishermen, miners, Indians, light-house keepers and even those who had turned their backs on society and now sought solitude along the cruel coast.

These sturdy souls on that tough little ship never complained—never found fault with their lot in life—never gave way to grumbling or gloom. The entire ship was alive, vibrant, dynamic with the great good fun those doughty seamen injected into their work for God and men. It was a tremendous lesson for me, starting out just then to seriously follow Christ no matter the cost.

Across the intervening years since then my Father has made it abundantly clear to me that one of His choicest gifts to His earth children is a quality of humor that helps and heals. There are few things of divine design which will do more to build bridges of goodwill between us and those whom we long to lead to Christ. The time to get deadly serious about spiritual issues will come more quickly if others can see us handle life's hard knocks with a touch of humor and the capacity to laugh at ourselves and our misfortunes. Few aspects of our lives show so clearly the serene strength of soul which comes to us from Christ.

Humor, fun, optimism have to be cultivated. They call for a deliberate act of the will; a determined choice of the mind and emotions to look for the light-hearted side of our days. At best they are few upon the earth, so it is wise to sprinkle them with laughter, fun and good cheer. Nothing else so quickly lifts the soul and heals the hurts.

Less than four hours after writing the preceding page there was an urgent long distance phone call. One of my dearest friends had suddenly been rushed to the hospital for major surgery. Only a week before his doctor had given him his annual medical check-up, declaring him to be fit as a fiddle. How would we face this together?

I leaped into my car and started off for the hospital at

high speed. It was late in the evening, but the nurses agreed to give me extra grace time after visiting hours since I was coming in from out of town. As I approached the city a battered old vehicle, towing a trailer load of trash, was creeping down the road. Swiftly I swept around the slow driver intent on reaching the hospital as soon as possible.

To my astonishment the slower old vehicle suddenly took life and tailgated me right into the hospital parking lot. When I stepped out of my car I was confronted by a very angry, very intoxicated man. His eyes blazed with hostility; his bright red mustache bristled with rage. He demanded to know why I had passed him so swiftly.

With an outpouring of expletives he tied into me in a rage. Quietly I placed my hand on his flailing arm and explained my mission of mercy so late in the evening. Suddenly his whole deportment changed. "Oh, sir!" he exclaimed, very crestfallen, "I was just trying to be a 'Good Samaritan!'" I had a hard time to keep from laughing out loud. "After all you know, sir, if the cops ever saw you pass me that way they would nail you with a $250.00 fine!"

I smiled at him warmly, and briefly we had a chuckle together. Then I gripped his outstretched hand, thanked him for his concern, and we parted in great good-will.

Quickly I gathered up the gorgeous Godetia my wife so lovingly sent along with me. She had bought it for our home just two days before. Then I rushed into the hospital just moments before closing time.

As I burst into my friend's room, as by a miracle he lifted his head from the pillow and shouted aloud, "Praise God—you have come, my friend!" All his roommates were astonished as we "old codgers" warmly embraced each other then exploded into gales of laughter as we so often do together. It was really not like a usual hospital room at all, for we shared joyfully in our mutual affection and good cheer. Even the nurse who came in was astonished.

He told me, grinning ear to ear, with only one old snag of a tooth showing starkly in his mouth, all about his conversation with the surgeon who would operate in the morning. He said, "I have already prayed earnestly for you, doctor. I have also prayed for all your staff and all your assistants. But now there is one more thing I wish you to know. You are going to operate on very precious property. For you see I belong to God, my Father, so be very, very careful what you do. This body does not belong to me. It belongs to Him!"

We had a hearty laugh over this. Then he showed me how he summoned help from the nurses. Not by pressing a button on the buzzer alarm, but by beating on his chest and distended torso, stretched tight like a drum. Again we were engulfed in gales of rib-stretching mirth. It was as if the whole room was filled with light.

Suddenly he turned to me very seriously and in a low voice whispered. "Phillip, do you think this good humor and mirth are appropriate in a place like this?" I looked into his eyes with great love and earnestness. Then I replied softly, "This is the special gift our Father has given you to touch all sorts of people in this place!"

There was no need to say more. He knew at once why he was there. A serene strength of soul lit up his countenance.

He gripped my hand hard. We prayed quietly together. As I rose to leave he said calmly, "The Lord's angel has visited me." All was well. It was enough.

His recovery has been remarkable!

And, always, always the simple, stunning statement he makes is *"The joy of the Lord is my strength!"*

So it can be for each of us.

There is absolutely no question about our Father's eager desire to have His children conquer the vicissitudes of life in the power of His might. Our strength of soul and buoyancy of spirit are bound up with His Spirit. We revel in His companionship and rest in the joyous assurance of His deliverance. In fact, we can laugh in the face of trouble!

It was Caleb of old who cried out that stirring, pulse-quickening challenge, *"Give me this mountain!"* even though he was a gnarled veteran of many years.

Each of us has his "mountains"! They come in all shapes and sizes. They stand before us as a challenge to our strength of soul, our serenity of spirit, our calm confidence in Christ.

And a large part of the secret for surmounting them, for turning "mountains into molehills," for casting them aside into the sea of no further remembrance is quiet trust in God Himself. Over and over He invites us to do this. His simple instruction, always, is, *"Trust Me. Trust Me!"*

The person who does this in simplicity of spirit, like a little child, possesses a unique and joyous attitude of mirth, good will and genial optimism. It is the attitude of the soul which removes mountains, not only from our own experience but also from the lives of others who seem unable to surmount them on their own.

Just two days ago Ursula and I went to call on a lady who had invited us to visit her. When we arrived she declined to see us because she was in such extraordinary pain. Her attendant said to come another day. I reassured her we would only stay a few brief moments if she would let us in.

She did!

The poor soul was writhing on her bed. Her eyes, with the awful suffering of her body, were filled with anguish and dark desperation. We spoke softly for just a few moments, then I asked for the privilege to pray for her. We bowed our heads humbly. Quietly I entreated Christ to touch her body and bring relief to her spirit. Then we left. It took no more than five minutes.

They next day she called in great jubilation. After our departure she had broken down completely in an outburst of weeping. Then suddenly there was an enormous release from her suffering. So that in truth and in fact God had given her the oil of joy for her mourning, the garment of praise in place of her spirit of heaviness.

Are you surprised that we too felt hilarious with joy and overflowing with praise to our Father? A very real mountain of anguish and agony had been removed. And all of us were brighter for it.

Yes, yes, yes! There is help, there is healing, there is hope in our lives when we have the wholesome good humor to take God seriously! Too many of us take the world too seriously. We take our troubles too seriously. We take the adversity of life too seriously.

It is when, with great good cheer, unshakeable courage, and high humor that we meet our challenges, we conquer them in the great authority of Christ. He resides in us. His resources are our resources. He actually laughs at His most formidable opponents. So should we! We must!

It is high time that Christians, at the close of this century, were less preoccupied with trying to find personal happiness and cheap entertainment in the church. It is high time they get to know Christ in the power of His resurrection life; that they can laugh at the forces of evil arrayed against them. Then in strength of soul they can go out to remove mountains in His might!

10

LIFTING
OTHER'S LOADS

One of the most compelling invitations ever extended by God to man came when Christ said quietly, *"Come unto Me, all ye that labor and are heavy laden, and I will give you rest."*

Perhaps as many people have come to Him in response to that call, as to any other statement He ever made. And we do not have to go far to find the reason why. Because almost every person we meet on the path of life actually does labor along with profound personal problems. They do carry heavy loads which weigh them down in despair and frustration and grief.

In saying that I am not referring so much to the struggles of earning a living, finding satisfactory employment, providing for one's family, facing ill health, or meeting the major reverses of life—including the adversity of stress. Rather I am satisfied Christ was fully aware of all the above, since He Himself had labored so long in the dusty carpenter's shop, and knew full well about bearing the heavy load of responsibility in providing for His widowed mother and His younger siblings.

Later on in life He had trudged back and forth across the trails of His native territory touching all kinds of people with all sorts of problems. He had fed the hungry. He healed those stricken with every sort of disease. He brought sight to the blind. He comforted those who mourned. He raised the dead. He dispelled demons and evil spirits. He brought comfort and cheer to all those who came to Him discouraged. Yes, He had lifted other's loads in scores of ways. As His followers He asks us to do the same.

The contemporary church, and twentieth century Christians, for the most part, have been generous in doing this work. All over the world, wherever they go, God's people have brought help, healing and hope to those who needed it. Too often the outstanding work done by dedicated men and women all over the world has been ignored, deliberately overlooked and even ridiculed by the media. This is simply because most members of the media have never come to Christ; they despise and reject Him; they prefer to rely on human schemes, governmental agencies and political pundits to solve social problems.

Still that should not deter each of us as God's children from doing his or her personal, private duty in lifting the loads of others in very practical ways. We can befriend the lonely. We can spend time with the sick. We can provide for the poor. We can share with those who sorrow. We can bring good cheer to those in despair. We can challenge the young ones to attempt great things for God.

In a hundred different ways, on a hundred different

days, we can do great good to bring kindness, love and mercy to struggling men and women. As has been said so often, *"We can be those in whom and through whom the Master still touches a thousand struggling souls."* We can be those who in truth, in sincerity, in practical, simple, humble service lift other's loads and so help bear their burdens.

But there is a dimension to life in which those around us are bound into a form of slavery and bondage that makes their existence a terrible struggle, and their loads of daily conduct are a cruel burden to bear. I am here referring to the inner struggles that rage within the soul. The dark, secret sins of the spirit estranged them from God our Father—the profound inner fever of searching for satisfaction that eludes most people. The pathos of having an outward show of success yet knowing full well the emptiness and ennui within. These are loads that most of us seldom try to lift. In fact we are afraid to even try. The task seems too daunting—too difficult.

Often this is because our own loads here have not been lifted. We ourselves have never come to Christ and found release in Him. We are not free from ourselves.

We have not yet found full satisfaction of soul.
We know nothing of the rest He offers us.
We have no strength of soul to lift other's loads.
We cannot share an abundant life we do not possess.

So we back away from those who come to us laboring to find freedom, broken down under the burdens of their own dreadful bondage. We prefer to send them to a pastor, a professional counselor, or even a psychologist or psychiatrist.

But there is a better way!
And we common people can help in lifting other's
    loads.

Allow me to recount an incident which occurred just last week to show exactly what is meant.

It was late Thursday evening when the phone rang. It was a long distance call from an agitated man down the valley. He was in anguish of spirit and deep distress of soul. He simply had to see me. They only reason he had thought of me was because he and his wife had come to several of the classes I taught in his community eight months before.

We agreed to meet privately in a little chapel in his village. As I drove down the next morning, there poured out from my soul a profound plea that he would have a vital, dynamic, personal encounter with Christ.

Quietly we sat side by side on the plain wooden pew at the very front of the sanctuary. It was cool, calm, and very still in the wee chapel. In a lovely way we were both enfolded with a powerful sense of Christ's presence. I just listened!

With absolute honesty, complete candor and unusual earnestness he poured out all of his life story. It was a tale of struggling, struggling to break free from the bondage of his own despicable behavior. He had joined a church. He had been baptized. He had read Christian books. He had listened to tapes. For nearly twenty years he had been active in the church. He thought he was a Christian and so did others. *But he was not!* He was still a slave to his own passions; addicted to his old desires; laboring under the wretched, killing load of his own personal selfishness and self-gratification.

The tragic tale poured from him in a torrent!

I did nothing to probe or pry into his past. I just listened!

But the Gracious Spirit of God was very active bringing this seeking soul from deep, deep conviction of sin and wrongdoing into a moving expression of godly sorrow.

Here was genuine repentance one seldom sees in our churches.

Again, and again, and again the dear man cried out to Christ for mercy, compassion, acceptance. Floods of tears cascaded down his checks. Bowed in spirit, contrite in heart, here was a soul begging to have his load lifted.

Without any complicated explanation, I simply assured him of two tremendous truths about Christ: *First— He is the One Who receives sinners. His assurance is: "Son, your sins are forgiven." Secondly—He is the One Who sets us free. Free from slavery to ourselves, free from serfdom to sin—free from serving Satan. Free from the fret of life to follow Him gladly.*

In the soft, subdued light of that village chapel this silver-haired gentleman in actual fact moved from the darkness of his despair into the lovely light of Christ's company. He who had struggled with the sins of his soul was set free to begin a brand new, abundant life as God's forgiven son. His load had been lifted.

The guilt was gone. The grime had been swept away in the cleansing, recreative touch of Christ's acceptance.

Tears of unabashed joy now replaced his remorse.

Gently but fervently we hugged. As we parted I said softly—"Go home and tell your wife what God has done for you."

That very evening, Friday night, the phone rang again. It, too, was a long distance call from down the valley. This time it was the man's wife. She simply had to see me. I offered to drive down and meet with her first thing the next morning.

At four A.M. on Saturday I awoke with a great, great concern for this couple. In intense earnestness of spirit I entreated Christ to meet with us in a life-changing encounter. All the way down the valley constant intercession poured from my soul.

This time I went to their humble little home, perched on a bench of land close up against a formidable rock bluff. I asked the man to go out for a stroll alone, while his wife spoke to me. In minutes I was aware that I was in the presence of a person whose whole disposition was as tough and stern and formidable as the gaunt, gray, granite bluff behind her house.

Her jaw was set hard. Her eyes smouldered with anger and hostility. Without apology she declared they really had no friends. Yet almost in the same breath she stated her whole life had been poured out in the church, for the church, to help the church. So again I simply sat quietly and listened! It would have to be Christ's Spirit who dealt with her hard and tough demeanor. It was obvious she considered herself a Christian. But as she rambled on it was astonishing how quickly she began to see she was not. I simply listened!

Bit by bit she began to be actually aware of her own terrible addiction to her own awful anger. She saw for the first time how she was chained to her own cruel criticism. Under the conviction of God's Gracious Spirit she discovered the beastly bitterness and vile jealousy that bound her in slavery.

Before my eyes, in a sudden, startling contrition of soul she began to weep and weep. Her husband had told me she could not cry.

That Saturday morning, in that humble home, the loads of a lifetime were lifted by the One who said, "Come unto me all ye that labor and are heavy laden and I will give you *rest!" Rest from your self. Rest from the shame and struggle of soul. Rest from sin and all its awful attitudes. Rest from Satan the deceiver.*

The "church goer," the "do-gooder," the "pretender" bowed in penitence and godly sorrow to receive Christ who alone could set her free. Free to admit her wrongs; free to cry out for mercy; free to accept God's forgiveness; free to know at last, at long last, she was truly, truly drawn into the family of our Father.

I went outdoors to find her husband. He had just returned. He came in quietly and all three of us sat together. Very softly but earnestly I explained to both of them exactly what had transpired. They exclaimed that never before had they understood what Christ could do. He had lifted their loads. He had set them free. They were fully forgiven! As children of God they could now, this very hour, begin a joyous, abundant new life in His company.

And they did!

Tears of pure joy poured from all our eyes.

Sheets and sheets of Kleenex were plucked from a box to try and staunch the streams.

They jumped to their feet, with remarkable agility for people so aged, and hugged me hard. Then they fell into each other's arms in an outpouring of affection one seldom sees!

This was a sacred moment in time.

And I knew we stood on a sacred spot.

It was also time for me to withdraw in awe and wonder.

As I drove home under the burning summer sun, the wind of God's Spirit swept anew into my spirit. All was well!

The reader may wonder why I have taken time to recount these incidents in such detail. There are two main reasons. The first is to show that there are in fact inner burdens that people everywhere bear. That these are severe struggles of soul which are seldom disclosed to others. Secondly, it is to point out that if we will allow ourselves to be used in simple ways, we can see Christ lift other's loads. We can share personally in the remarkable joy that comes to those set free.

When Christ declares that He comes to set the prisoners free; to give those in despair beauty for ashes; to provide a song of praise in place of the spirit of heaviness; this tremendous emancipation is what He is speaking about.

Too many Christians consider "sharing the great good news" a duty—something done under duress with great difficulty and much hesitancy. But for those of us who have found Christ's forgiveness and wondrous freedom for ourselves, it is a pure pleasure to introduce others to Him. We can do this in utter sincerity and loving concern. This is how we have a small part in lifting other's loads.

The beautiful bonus that our Father bestows on us is

that of jubilant good will within our own souls. This is how we are strengthened in our own faith, energized in our own intimate communion with Christ. No matter what you do to lift another's load, it is guaranteed your own soul will be strengthened and inspired. God is like that.

11

THE HUMILITY OF
DIMINISHED STRENGTH

We people of the so-called "western world" at the close of the twentieth century cannot be considered a humble society. We are known the world over for our wealth, our power, our extravagant life style, our boasting about the highest standard of living on earth, our computer technology, our preoccupation with power, pleasure and business prestige.

I believe all of this will alter drastically during the twenty-first century. Pride always comes before disaster. And our society, which has deliberately rejected the laws and principles ordained by God for human well being, is bound to go into decline. Our civilization will collapse from its own corruption as has every other great civilization in human history—basically because men and women will not humble themselves in the time of their decline. They refuse to seek their own renewal in the resources of God Himself. Instead, they rely increasingly on human

strength and wisdom only to collapse in chaos and corruption.

What happens to nations and civilizations likewise
happens in the individual's own life. Yet surprisingly few
people understand the principle. The world outlook, the
world preoccupation with wealth, the world search for
"success," the world emphasis on personal pride eclipse
the profound principle Christ enunciated when He was
here, namely,

*"A man's life does not consist in the abundance of his
possessions. A man's strength does not lie in his success."*

But we simply do not agree with Him.
   We are sure to think that way is stupid.
      Because everything we have been taught is the
      opposite.

We are completely convinced by our culture that what
we actually own or possess is a sure measure of our
strength. In that list of possessions are such things as
wealth, health, education, employment, prestige, pleasure,
fame, name, stamina, security and acquired skills.

The end result is that we have come not only to
regard those things we own as a criteria of our strength
but also as the very source of our strength. Herein lies
one of the greatest and most pervasive of our delusions as
a people. It is a deception of monumental proportions
that has trapped millions of human beings. Accompany-
ing this false outlook on life is the pride, aggressiveness
and greed which are all part of the accumulation of possessions.

To reverse this process our Father in His concern for

us arranges our human strength and our human resources to be diminished. This painful procedure is not intended to diminish or destroy our delight in life. Rather, it is meant to humble our haughtiness and to drive us in earnestness to seek enduring strength of soul in Himself.

It is one thing to state this in words.
It is quite another to know this severe lesson in life.
And most people prefer to pass by it, if possible.

In the scriptural record we find God's Gracious Spirit recording the procedure for us in vivid word pictures. Time after time those who were chosen for special purposes by God were first diminished and humbled.

Three classical accounts are those of Job, Jacob and Moses.

It was Job who was stripped of his health, his wealth and his family who ultimately found his great strength in God. It was he who declared without apology, *"Even though He slay me—still I shall trust Him."*

Jacob, the schemer, was sure he could survive on the basis of his accumulated wealth. But God met the man, touched his thigh, crippled his conceit, and drove him to find his strength in the Living God.

Moses, a prince in Egypt with all the privileges and power of the court, was forced to flee to the desert. There he met God in poverty and found a new strength in Him.

This is why Paul stated bluntly, *"When I am weak, then I am strong—for my strength is made perfect (mature—complete) in weakness."* This is what Christ Himself meant when He said simply, *"The least shall be the greatest in the Kingdom of God."*

Most of us have been baffled by such contradictions. We consider them a *conundrum.* We are puzzled and perplexed by such a paradox.

Partly that is because we do not understand the essential and basic character of Christ Himself. His very nature is one of enormous generosity. He gives and gives and gives of Himself in order to bless and benefit others. His never-ending self-sharing bestows endless benefits upon us, whether we deserve them or not. We call this His *grace.*

Yet we human beings, for the most part, live out our little lives in just the opposite way. We insist on our own self-aggrandizement. We are preoccupied with our own selfish self-interests. We pursue our own possessions; we pander to our own pride; we parade our own prestige.

Then we wonder why there is no harmony between us and Him. We are startled to discover He resists the proud person.

It is not until a man or woman experiences first hand the painful process of diminishing strength that humility of the soul, heart (will), and contrition of spirit set into the life. It is no easy, simple process.

But the splendid result is that we then learn that *"The Lord is nigh (close) unto them that are of a broken heart (subdued will); and saveth such as be of a truly contrite (penitent) spirit."*

It is such a soul with whom Christ loves to keep company. And, it is in His companionship we find strength of soul! His strength becomes mine.

Perhaps if I here recount very briefly my own spiritual saga in being humbled by "The Most High," the reader will grasp the principle clearly. At least it is worth the try.

As a young man I had become very haughty because of my superb scientific training. My academic arrogance led me to believe that the application of scientific technology could solve the problems not only of society as a whole, but my own in particular. *This view is rampant all over the world.*

By pursuing that path vigorously I not only ignored God, but came to the conclusion He did not even need to be consulted. In very large measure I made all my own decisions and carved out my own career, confident that my skills, my expertise, my enormous drive would guarantee "success"—as the world counts success.

The end result was that despite great poverty in my youth, and with no special "contacts," my career as a consultant and advisor to both government and industry was astonishing. My associates marveled at the manner in which my endeavors prospered.

So much so that by the time I was twenty-seven years old I had great dreams of owning my own ranch and being financially independent by the age of thirty. I came within a hair of doing just that. I purchased one of the most lovely oceanfront estates I have ever seen: 214 acres of glorious property with over two miles of beautiful ocean shore line. I was sure I was set for life. It became *my strength—my source of security—my inspiration.*

Suddenly one spring morning, several years later, federal agents drove up to my house and announced that it was all being taken as a major military base for the navy. In a single drastic stroke of divine arrangement I was stripped of my strength, my security, my inspiration.

This haughty man had been humbled into the dust at His feet.

For the first time in many years I turned earnestly to
Christ in my extremity. Shattered, broken in spirit, devas-
tated about a fractured future, I sought strength, solace
and security in God Himself. He did not disappoint me.
He did give me fresh hope, new life, even wider vistas. He
is just that way when we truly seek Him with all our soul.

But I was a slow learner when it came to spiritual
principles. Soon I was caught up in another compelling
career as an ecological consultant to the Kenya government in East Africa. My life was an enormous adventure
as I virtually lived on safari in Masai territory. Lions,
leopards, elephants, rhino and buffalo became an integral
part of my life, just as did the free-spirited Masai who
were my friends.

I was sure that with my energy, my enthusiasm, my
skills, my strength, there would be a boundless future on
the sweeping lion-colored plains of my beloved homeland.
Then suddenly, silently, swiftly I was stricken with severe
illness. Even the best of medical doctors could not diag-
nose my condition. Their prognosis was that I had less
than six months left to live. The only remote chance of
recovery was to leave the tropics. So, again, broken, shattered, stripped of strength, I returned to Canada's cool
and healing shores.

In my utter despair once again I turned to Christ, my
great physician, and begged for restoration. He heard my
cry and without medical aid renewed my strength again.

The years went by in wondrous ways. My books were
accepted with enthusiasm. I began to lecture on resource
conservation. I undertook major wildlife film production.
Again my star was rising, and all seemed serene and
sure. Then it happened like a thunderclap. Phyllis, my

beloved, was stricken with terrible, incurable cancer. Two years later she died in my arms and was gone. And I was spent.

It is at times like these of diminished strength that the soul can only find its support in God Himself.

God's ways are not our ways.
Few of us understand His ways.
We are baffled when He strips us to strengthen us.
It seems such a contradiction in terms.
We recoil from the procedure.
But this is the path to strengthen the soul.

If we are truly sensitive in spirit to His Spirit we will begin to see this concept clearly in all of life. Perhaps it is most apparent in our diminishing physical strength; in the gradual slowing of reflexes; in the steady decrease of energy and vitality; in the slower footsteps. We are faced with a crucial series of choices. Will we give way to despair, bitterness and self-pity? Or will we turn to our Father and find in Him widening vistas, and new resources of divine design that can enrich our days and inspire others?

Hanging on the wall of my office is a prayer which states this in part—

"O Lord, keep me reasonably sweet;
I do not want to be a sour old saint—
Some of them are so hard to live with . . .
Give me the ability to see good in unexpected places,
And the lovely talents in unexpected people.
And, give me, O Lord, the grace to tell them so!
Amen."

As the years go by we can become bitter or better.
We can likewise become bored or bright.
We can become mad or glad.

The choices are ours. If we lash out at life, railing in anger against our reduced human resources, we become bitter. On the other hand in humility of spirit we can seek Christ's companionship, finding renewed vitality and new vistas. We can discover a new dimension of delight to our days.

David, that remarkable and illustrious poet, put it this way:

"I will go out in the strength of the Lord God;
I will make mention of Thy righteousness . . .
O God, Thou hast taught me from my youth: . . .
Hitherto have I declared Thy wondrous works.
Now, also, when I am old and grayheaded.
O God, forsake me not until I have
shewed Thy strength unto this generation, . . .
And Thy power to everyone that is to come."
Psalm 71:16-18

This is the heart cry of a humble heart. This is the inner passion of the person stripped of pride; stripped of power; stripped of prestige. Yet, that same soul has found strength, energy and zest in Christ, the Lord of His life. It is this divine dimension of partaking of God's own being which can bestow strength of soul into all of our years.

Those of us who have discovered this secret source of new vitality with which to face the vicissitudes of life are not easily discouraged by the specter of diminishing vitality. Quite the opposite, we meet the challenges with good cheer because He is here. We do not pretend to be hot-headed young people with all the stamina of youth. We calmly acknowledge our limitations, then proceed, with God's help, to accomplish the work He assigns us without fuss or fret.

We learn the humble art of prayer in our projects. We are lowly enough to seek guidance from God and not just from man. We do not parade our accomplishments but prefer to heap honor on Him. For He is our strength. He is our delight. He is *the Initiator* behind the scenes.

So it is that even all of life with Him is an adventure.
We expect life to be charged with excitement.
Yet we also find it replete with quiet contentment.
Because He shares His magnificent strength with us.

What an abundant life He lavishes on His own.

12

SIMPLICITY OF LIFE EASES THE WAY

O ver and over the comment is made, *"Life is so complicated!"* Or again and again people remark, *"There is nothing easy these days!"* Even more often people burst out in frustration: *"Why don't they simplify things for a change?"*

These are legitimate observations on the complexity of our twentieth century life style in the western world. In large part they spring out of our insatiable demands for ease, luxury, pleasure, comfort and convenience. They are such an integral part of our commercial world with its great emphasis on consumer demand that we accept the frenzy of accumulating things as the core of our culture.

Most of us have no clear concept of just how relentless are the pressures put upon us to simply "pile it up." We rush about in a fever of frantic activity, much like Chipmunks or Squirrels gathering up a stockpile of seeds against the threat of winter weather. We are completely convinced that *"more is better."* Somehow we are sure this is the supreme secret to success, security or sensual pleasure. So we push on in our mad scramble wondering why we are worn out and jaded by what we thought would bring us joy.

I have a friend who took early retirement four years ago. Just two weeks ago he and his wife looked so tired and drawn that in sincere concern I inquired if they were well. Their reply astonished me. "When we retired we looked forward so much to a less hectic life. Instead we seem to be so, so busy, that by the end of the day we are both worn out. All we want to do is put our feet up and fall asleep."

What is the problem?

In a word it is their "possessions."

Standing in their large and lovely yard are the following: A luxurious car; a camper van; a large and powerful motorbike; a utility trailer; a travel trailer; a pleasure cruiser; a fishing boat.

The gentleman is fastidious about keeping all this complex equipment in first class condition. He spends hours and hours every week in cleaning, polishing, repairing and general maintenance of this mechanical gadgetry. One day, while servicing the motor in the cruiser, he remarked to me with a sigh, "Paying for the upkeep of this pleasure craft is like pouring water in a pail that has a huge hole in it! There is simply no end to the cost of owning it."

His wife has exactly the same difficulty with her attractive garden, her beautiful shrubs and endless array of ornamental house plants. She just keeps adding and adding to the collection. And with each new acquisition the load of care increases.

The answer to all this may seem easy.
Just get rid of half the stuff.
But it is not that simple.

Because beneath it all lies the much more profound matter of one's priorities in life.

Why does a man accumulate mechanical equipment? He loves it. Why does a woman plan and plant a most elaborate garden? She loves it.

So the difficult decisions in simplifying life are not just to do with selling off what we own or tearing up the precious things we planted or collected. The tough choices have to do with what do I love? What do I enjoy? What panders to my personal pride or pleasure or performance?

As our years slip softly into memories, there is a need to pause and ask ourselves some very hard questions. Do I really need all this stuff for a fully satisfying life? Is this really the best way to spend the years that remain? Are there less complicated means to relish my days, yet at the same time have energy to expend on others? Is it possible to switch priorities so that both I and those around me find life easier?

The reader is entreated not to think that "things" in themselves are evil. They are not! It is what place they occupy in our priorities which poses the problem and complicates our commitments to them. The same identical principle applies to any other interest which demands and commands our thought, time, strength and devotion. These may be as diverse as our careers, our business, our hobbies, our homes, our leisure activities, travel, sports or even our money.

Each or any of these can actually possess a person.
  Once they become the prominent goal they drive us.
    We are no longer our own, but held captive by
      them.
      This produces enormous tension and stress in
        life.

It is what complicates our choices within.
  Christ Himself said we cannot serve two masters.
    Our loyalty and love is to one or the other.

Most Christians are caught in a complex maze just
here. Because from their childhood they have been conditioned by their culture to believe "more is better"; the
"bigger the better"; "go for broke"; "get ahead of the rest."
Even their pastors, preachers and teachers hand them
the same line.

But that is not the path to inner peace.
  It is not the secret to quiet strength of soul.
    Nor does it ever satisfy the soul and spirit.

Christ gave us the simple solution to simplifying life.
It is just this: "*Seek ye first (as an absolute priority) the
kingdom of God (the control of Christ in life) and His righteousness (right relationships with God and men), then all
these other things (other interests) shall be added unto you
(bestowed on you)*" *(Matthew 6:33).*

Most of us simply do not believe this statement.

We will not live by this spiritual principle.

We reject it out of hand as impractical and unwork-
able.

Almost exactly twenty-two years ago, to this very day,
on a remote, wind-blown beach in Australia, where I was

stricken with a massive heart seizure I wrote these simple lines:

"The longer I live, the more keenly I am aware that basically all that counts in life is what we can contribute of comfort, cheer, and inspiration to others. The success of our living is measured not by what we can accumulate for ourselves, but by what we can bestow upon our fellow travelers on life's tough trail" (from *Taming Tension,* now published as *Serenity*).

In those difficult days it seemed unlikely I would even survive the next six months. In His compassion and patient care my Father has granted me twenty-two more years to serve His people and His interests on earth in as simple and straightforward a way as possible. It has not been easy to do this, governed by God Himself, under the supreme sovereignty of His Spirit.

Many, many people misunderstand the motives.
They challenge the concept of complete commitment to Christ.
They scorn the simplicity of this sort of life style.

This is the way Jesus of Nazareth—The Christ of God—lived and behaved when He was here among us. He declared without apology that it was a narrow (constricted) way, for it called for total commitment to Himself and His view of life. He did not hesitate to warn us that few would ever find it within their wills to choose this way to live, much less follow in His footsteps.

For this is the path of self-sacrifice, self-denial, self-giving!

It is just the opposite way from the world's way of selfishness, self-gratification and self-aggrandizement.

Yet the person who chooses Christ's simplicity finds rest of spirit and serenity of soul.

He assured us this would be so. Because it is His presence, His power, His peace within that empowers us to tramp out the tough trail with ease and courage in His company.

For reasons not easily explained or understood by me, it has been part of my life to visit many patients in many hospitals. Ever since my first wife died by degrees, over a period of two full years, from terminal cancer, hospitals have had a stark horror for me. They are a grim and ghastly reminder of the dreadful ordeal we endured as Phyllis went in and out of them thirteen times before she and I were released from her awful agony.

Yet calling on people in these places of pain has been a large part of my life during the past twenty years. Why, why, why? Simply because that is the path Christ calls me to follow. I could be stubborn, self-willed and refuse to go. But that would only complicate the inner contortions of my own conscience. It would deny others the compassion of Christ. And all of us would be poorer for it.

There are lovely compensations in all of this. Christ has His wondrous ways of making up to us for our devotion. He is no man's debtor. All of which eases the way for all of us.

Yesterday I was in a neighboring village when I felt constrained to go to the hospital to see an elderly patient. It was mid-morning, a time when visitors are not allowed in. I went to the information desk and asked if I could leave a note. To my astonishment the nurse asked, "Why don't you just go in?" I came to the nursing station and a pleasant lady smiled and assured me it would be fine to go in for a few moments.

I found the patient alone in a darkened room. The dear fellow was in deep distress of soul, discouraged in spirit, suffering severely. With surprising frankness he unburdened himself to me.

Quietly I assured him again of our Father's care for him. We prayed together. We wept together. We held hands together.

As we parted, His presence permeated that place of pain.

The patient's eyes brimmed over with glistening tears of quiet joy and strength of soul.

"Phillip," he remarked softly, "you are the one visitor who calls on me in trouble, and leaves me with renewed life surging up within!"

That single, simple statement was compensation enough for all the scores and scores of soul-wrenching hospital calls made across the years. Not just for him, but for me as well, it was the strength of soul which makes life easier, brighter, buoyant! And that strength comes from Christ Himself.

The secret to this sort of service to God and man is a singleminded determination to do our Father's will no matter the personal cost involved. It is this quiet, sincere, simple objective to be absolutely available to Christ and His cause that cuts through all the confusion and complexity of our century and our culture.

Christ Himself set His noble face like a flint to go to Calvary, to His terrible suffering, to His awful agony on behalf of a perishing world. His single, simple, uncomplicated end in life was to do His Father's will.

Because He did, millions upon millions of us poor, stumbling, struggling sinners have been born again, remade and redeemed from destruction! It cost Him the cross, and He asks us as His followers to take up our crosses daily if we wish to walk in His company.

This call to self-denial and self-sacrifice on His behalf and for the sake of others who are lost does not set well with many today—nor at any time in history. People prefer to play around. It is much more appealing to pick up our wealth in whatever form it takes. It is more fun to pursue pleasure and pass our time in pointless pursuits. *"Life is short—play hard!"* is the world's way today.

All sorts of books, seminars and lectures are now being offered to the public on "How to Simplify Life." There seems to be an inner soul hunger among us to get back to the basics. Large numbers of people are turning away from their infatuation with our much vaunted technology and the multiplicity of gadgets and gimmicks that earmark our affluent society.

But going back to bicycles or eating only organic foods or living off the land will not nourish the deep inner longings of the human spirit nor satisfy the intense thirst of soul which consumes many of our contemporaries. Only Christ can do this. For it is only the Spirit of God Himself who can adequately assuage the inner yearning of our own spirits. And we remain restless until this happens.

Our Lord spoke to this point in simple language without apology. He stated in the plainest possible terms: "I Am the bread of life—He that eats (partakes) of Me will never hunger for soul satisfaction again. I Am the water of life—He who drinks (imbibes) of Me shall never thirst again."

A few of us have found these facts to be utterly true.

And in that finding all of life has suddenly been simplified. As Paul put it, "For me to live is Christ!" The supreme secret is "Christ in you—you in Christ."

When this happens it is no hardship to dispose of the multiplicity of other interests, activities or possessions which may have cluttered our lives and complicated our days. We do not find it beyond us to part with our possessions, our play times, our pride or our preferences in order to touch perishing people all around us.

We have found our strength of soul in the Living Son of God. We have found our spirits soaring in simple response to His Spirit. We have found the single supreme center of life in our Father's care and company. *And life is easier!*

13
REFUSE TO WORRY

The dawn of the morning on which I turned 65 years of age my soul was in intimate communion with Christ. It was a landmark occasion for me. Again and again across the long and often difficult years of my life I had wondered to myself if I would even reach my 60th birthday. My Dad had died at 54. Mother had gone home at 64. And my own health had been so fragile for so many years. So it seemed an early demise would not be a surprise.

Now suddenly here I was at the dawn of my 65th birthday in greater strength and more robust health than I had known in years and years. It seemed I stood on the threshold of a brand new epic in life—that stage called *"old age."* As the door opened to this chapter of unknown duration what should I do with the days, months or years left to me?

I am not too shy to discuss such things with Christ. He has become my closest confidante, my dearest companion, my most respected mentor. In audible language, articulated aloud in the privacy of our close communion, I asked Him to make clear to me the most essential, most important principle I should adhere to as I entered the so-called "twilight years."

I was not seeking some secret of ease or comfort with which to spend my remaining time. I had decided long ago that with my Father's faithfulness, the closing chapter in life could be just as productive, just as buoyant, just as worthwhile as those chapters of middle life.

But what was the supreme secret for me as a man?

The deep inner response which came to me that morning from Christ's Spirit was absolutely unmistakeable. Just two short commands: As emphatic as if spoken aloud.

"Refuse to worry!"—"Just trust Me!"

That may sound very simple.

But it is extremely difficult.

Especially for a man trained to plan his own life. We of the western world are taught to take great thought for tomorrow . . . to fine tune everything for the future.

Could a person my age suddenly change his personal conduct from one of trying to cover every contingency—to that simple outlook of not worrying at all and quietly trusting God for every area in life? There and then I determined with God's power I would set my soul to do so. I declared audibly, in an act of calm faith, that from that hour on I refused to worry. . . . Instead, just trust Him!

I faced this formidable mountain of anxiety that had loomed so large in my life for so many years. It had cast its dark shadow over my days in various ways. Here are but a few worries common to most of us.

Fretting over the unknown future.
Concern about the welfare of my family.
The stress of meeting social obligations.
Distress over fragile health and strength.

The uncertainty of adequate income in inflation.
Meeting other's expectations.
The possible collapse of our civilization.

These are but seven samples of the innumerable issues over which most of us fret and worry, plan and prepare for the unknown. We delude ourselves often when we say we do not worry. The terrible truth is most of us do not trust Christ. It is true we may trust Him for our spiritual salvation, and a few trust Him for their sanctification.

But the majority of us *worry our way through the world.*

I was determined that with Christ's companionship, I would adamantly, deliberately, refuse to worry any more.

I crossed the great divide of doubt. I entered into the "rest" He offers.

I was set free from fretting!
What a glorious emancipation!

There are two sides to this great deliverance. On the one hand it is our Father's desire that we should actually relish and repose in the *rest* He provides. On the other, there must be a deep and determined desire on our part to partake of the peace of mind and serenity of soul He offers us.

This calls for steadfast faith in our Father and in His generous commitments to His children. It is not enough merely to "hope" He will help us. It is essential to state our confidence aloud to others around us. It is important to be bold enough to state audibly that we refuse to worry, choosing rather to trust God.

The Lord Jesus Christ gave us very clear directions in this. He stated, *"Have faith in God!"* or *"Have the faith of God."* *"For verily I say unto you,"* Jesus said, *"that whosoever shall say unto that mountain (of worry)—'be thou removed, and be thou cast into the sea' (of forgetfulness); and shall not doubt in his heart, but shall believe that those things which he* saith, *shall come to pass; he shall have whatsoever he saith"* (Mark 11:22-28).

Please note this powerful promise is predicated upon a person actually articulating, in an audible voice, what he believes God can do. The reason for stating our faith in our Father and declaring our confidence in Christ is to announce our calm assurance in Christ to others around us.

This is not an act of bravado, but of simple obedience to Christ's command. It is not staged showmanship to try to impress others. Rather, it is a plain declaration that "I refuse to worry"! Instead, "I trust God!"

Spurgeon, in one of his classic statements, put it plainly:

"Blessed and fortunate are they who have a simple faith in Jesus Christ, intertwined with deep affection for Him. This is a restful confidence. These lovers of Jesus are charmed with His character and delighted with His mission (instructions). They are carried along by the loving-kindness that He has manifested. Therefore they cannot help trusting Him because they so much admire, revere, and love Him. . . .

"We love Him and He loves us. So we put ourselves

into His hands, accept whatever He prescribes, and *do whatever he bids*. We know that nothing can be wrongly ordered while He is the director of our affairs. He loves us too well to let us perish or suffer a single needless pang. . . .

"Steadfast faith is the root of obedience. This may be clearly seen in the affairs of life. . . . So faith which refuses to obey the commands of the Savior is a mere pretence and will never save the soul!"

The above declaration may be couched in rather archaic language. Yet it is as sure and solid as one can state it. The terrible tragedy is that very few of God's children live this way. I was one of them for long, long years of my younger life.

I literally worried my way through the world.
I fretted and fumed over every frustration.
I fought for every advantage against every adversary.
I knew little about faith, even less about rest.
I knew all about struggle and weariness of soul.

Then Christ in His mercy and grace came to me with His outstretched arms and gentle invitation. *"Refuse to worry . . . just trust Me!"* Take no thought for tomorrow.
Just take me for tomorrow!

To worry is to doubt the credibility of Christ to care for us.
To worry is to focus our attention on circumstances.
To worry is to center our thoughts on our cares.
To worry is to imagine a crisis before it comes.
So it must be asked, *"How does one refuse to worry?"*

There are four powerful aspects to this relationship with our Father which must be cultivated if we are ever to trust Him fully. They are basic to believing Him.

1)   *Get to Know God.*

The better we understand His true character the more we respect, love and trust Him. I am not speaking about the doctrines or dogma expounded by theologians and scholars. I am referring to the plain record of His dealing with the human race all through human history. It is given to us common people to read carefully and reflect upon seriously.

Spend time in the Scriptures. Ruminate quietly over the remarkable record of God's faithfulness, patience, kindness and generosity to those who trusted Him and obeyed His commands. It is an astonishing disclosure of mercy, compassion, care and grace toward us men.

This is the essential character of our Father. It is displayed in its most brilliant colors in the life of our Lord Jesus Christ. Read and re-read the story of His short sojourn among us. Get to know Him first hand by how He behaved; how He befriended sinners; how He cared so profoundly for those in pain; how He delivered those in distress; how He understood people fully; how He gave Himself gladly in great strength to deliver us; how He forgives so freely.

As a person begins to know Christ in terms of His character and His conduct, it becomes increasingly more reasonable and more inviting to take the second step.

2)   *Submit (yield) Yourself to Him.*

Perhaps an even better word is *entrust* your entire life to our Father's care and control.

The modern church, sad to say, does not say much about this actual surrender or abandonment of ourselves to Christ. The current evangelical emphasis is *"Invite Christ into your life"* as though you, a mere mite of humanity, are doing God a great favor by opening the door of your life to Him.

The essential step a person must ultimately take is to deliberately place himself or herself and all one possesses under Christ's command. This demonstrates that we have come to know a little of the grandeur and generosity of The Most High and so are prepared to entrust everything to Him.

We call this capitulation, "Coming under Christ's control"; "Giving ourselves over to the government of God"; "Submitting ourselves to the sovereignty of His Spirit."

In short, by a deliberate act of the will, and choice of soul, one decides to give all of himself and all of his future to God . . . to be at His disposal.

This is a stupendous surrender. Few people ever do it. Most Christians gladly entrust their so-called "salvation" to Christ as an insurance policy against perdition. But not one in a hundred entrust all their daily interests, activities, pursuits and pleasures to Him as a guarantee of serenity of spirit or strength of soul to triumph today, and triumph tomorrow.

Christ said plainly, *"Come to Me and you will find rest."* Most of us in our pride prefer to worry our own way through this weary old world.

3) *Having Come to Christ—Just Trust Him.*

If we are in earnest about this intimate relationship with The Living God, it calls for calm confidence in His character that He can fully care for *me*. He becomes *my* "caretaker"!

The word "caretaker," is used here with great sincerity and respect. Not just in the sense of one who "serves" others, though Christ has become a "servant," "a minister" for our sakes. But I use it in the much more powerful dimension of Him being the One who can provide for us, protect us, and empower us to live in peace, purity and strength of soul.

We are told very explicitly to cast all our cares upon Him, for He cares for us. Most of us simply don't believe Him. We are burdened down with all our own baggage. We fret and fume and fight ferociously with every frustration.

Surely, surely, if Christ is "The Perfect Gentleman," as I have found Him to be, simple reason should enable me to see it is the highest honor to quietly trust Him with all that touches my life. And I do, day by day, hour by hour! In that calm confidence there lies great repose and sweet serenity of spirit because of this new dimension of delight.

4)   *Humbly Obey Him.*

To comply with Christ's commands is to demonstrate without a shred of doubt that I am loyal to Him and love Him deeply. He Himself stated this fact over and over.

We delude ourselves and deceive others if we claim to be Christ's followers while at the same time refusing to comply with His wishes or carry out His will—and worry, worry, worry.

Again this is why it is imperative to spend much time in His Word, to become familiar first hand with His will,

His way and His work. When I know Him well and understand clearly His instructions, I will discover it is an honor not a hardship to carry them out—a delight not a drudgery!

His commands are in fact His royal commitments to me. It is as I step out in quiet faith to carry out His wishes, He empowers me to so act. He makes good on His commitments. He provides plenty for my poverty—serenity for my strife—power for my weakness—wondrous joy for my old worries. Bless Him forever!

14

INSPIRATION
OUT-OF-DOORS

It may sound strange to the reader, yet it is a well known fact that an excellent antidote to worry is to walk. Just getting outdoors, away from the usual, immediate surroundings of home or office can work wonders in our outlook if we will let it do so.

Join another friend or family member if you wish, but preferably walk alone, only in company with Christ, if you seek refreshment of spirit and strength of soul from above. I say this in the utmost sincerity, because then there are fewer distractions from the primary purpose of the walk—finding inspiration in the natural world, created with such care by our Father.

Twenty-five years ago, in a secular book on outdoor conservation; which became a best seller, I wrote the following comment. "It has been well said that *'Walking is a lost art on this continent!'* Cars and trucks, trains and planes, motor scooters and powered snow toboggans have supplanted sturdy legs and strong lungs. More than that, though, they have torn from us the thrill offered by a tranquil tramp across country, or the serenity of a gentle stroll taken in solitude or with a close companion."

Fortunately the intervening years have seen a significant change in our society in this area of physical activity. So much so that millions upon millions of people now walk for the sake of their health. To my amazement a high quality, carefully edited, monthly magazine now comes to my home entitled simply, *"Walking."*

This increased interest in walking is highly commendable. Unfortunately, the emphasis on the exercise is largely physical in nature. People are encouraged to walk for the purpose of bodily health, increased stamina and the toning of muscles and tendons. There is, however, a profound and delightful dimension to walking outdoors that has much to do with our mental health and spiritual well-being.

Walking is not just a matter of getting from A to B, then back again. It is much more than covering so many miles in so many minutes. It goes far beyond burning up so many calories in energy expenditure. It even surpasses the benefits of a sturdy constitution or slim, trim body. It can become the source of inspiration of spirit and strength of soul for the child of God who seeks renewal out-of-doors.

A walk out-of-doors, to be fully rewarding, demands much more than just the exercise of legs and lungs. It involves the use of eyes, ears and more—even the senses of touch and taste. Beyond all of these lies the acute sense of *"seeing"* with the soul and spirit; holding oneself open to the inspiration and uplift of surroundings, attentive to the mood and music of the infinite.

It is this art of responding to the clear flowing stream of spiritual stimulation that flows to us from our Father in the natural world around us which works wonders in our lives. Last evening I took my grandson for a short tramp down a nearby stream. He is a strong, sturdy 16-year old lad, six feet tall and built like a bull. For the most part his whole life is trucks, power equipment and electrical gadgets. But for an hour I introduced him into a whole new realm.

We stopped to watch the Trout hanging steady in the clear, swift running stream. Now and then a large Carp would cast his shadow over the stones in the riverbed. We paused to pluck wild Choke Cherries from the laden bushes where Bohemian Waxwings banqueted on the fruit. We walked softly along the stony trail and listened quietly to the song of the rapids. We marveled at the multi-colored hues of green, blue, silver and white that the powerful current produced in its surge down the valley.

For a few precious moments the man-made world of motors and machinery and strident sounds was closed out. All was still.

In that stillness there was also serenity.
Indelible impressions were being etched on the lad's soul and mine.
These were memorable moments to be treasured.
But it took time, thought and attention to shape them.
Besides all these is the adventure of new surprises.

Several days ago I went for a quiet stroll in an open, park-like pine forest. It was new terrain for me in a range of rock-ribbed hills above a shining upland lake. It had rained for several days, so my footsteps were totally silent on the damp vegetation and dark wet soil. I moved like a wraith through the woods.

Suddenly, just as I broke out of the trees at timber line a lovely Nighthawk lifted from the forest floor in front of me. Swiftly, softly, silently the dark bird, with such long graceful wings, settled down among some boulders and began to feign it had a broken wing. Then it began to cry plaintively, pretending it was seriously injured. All this ploy was to distract my attention from where she had been brooding her mottled eggs.

I was sure I could find them if I searched long enough. To my unbounded surprise I found them, not in a nest at all, not even in a formed hollow on the ground, but simply lying side by side on the mat of pine needles beneath a small tree. In all my life I had never seen such a casual, carefree sort of arrangement, for a species to perpetuate its kind upon the planet. No nest, no shelter, no camouflage!

Yet here was a magnificent bird that had thrilled me for forty years. Its swift, deft flight could outdo any insect on the wing: The dramatic, dizzying power dives that reverberated in the evening twilight with "K-A-Z-O-O": and its spectacular courting displays all aroused my admiration.

And at the same time these birds survived and succeeded from generation to generation all without undue concern or care for even a nest.

Like an electrical charge of high voltage energy and uplift the thought swept through my entire being—"our Father cares for Nighthawk chicks on the forest floor. He can care for you as well!" In wonder, awe and inspiration I stood still, alert, but also subdued in spirit, gazing down at two large, light-brown eggs, beautifully mottled on their bed of pine needles.

Yes, yes, yes! If God could care so well for wild birds on this bare-boned, rugged, rock ridge, He could also care for me amid the mayhem and madness of man's modern world. Are you surprised that there was a spring in my step, a song in my spirit, and strength in my soul as I headed for home?

That is the sort of enthusiasm *(En – Theo = in God)* to be found in the humble art of walking. Our attention is turned away from self-interest to those phenomena of the glorious natural world around us—if we will allow it to happen. More importantly, if we set our wills to seek His presence in the common places around us.

Taking a quiet stroll outdoors can be seen as a treasured rendezvous with our dearest friend Christ Himself. Often, often, His presence is so poignant, so pervasive in a setting of trees, fields, a garden, beside a stream or on a mountain ridge that I must pause to relish the moment. As a man living at the end of the twentieth century, I am acutely aware of the enormous ecstasy and awe which swept over Mary Magdalene all alone in the garden on the resurrection morning. In that eternal encounter with The Living Lord Jesus Christ she could only exclaim, *"Rabboni!"—"Master!"*

He has not changed across the intervening centuries.
　　He still comes to those of us who seek Him earnestly.
　　He speaks in ways not audible to our physical

senses, but just as convincing and clear to
our inner souls.
He assures us just as surely that *"He is alive."*
   He supplies us with spiritual strength in
      restoration, in renewal, in resurrection
      might.

It has frequently astonished me that Christians often
do not walk.

In striking contrast it is surprising how many play
golf, go skiing, play tennis or take long car trips for recre-
ation. All of these activities are very expensive. There are
endless costs for elaborate equipment, special clothing,
fees and travel expenses.

Walking outdoors is absolutely free, except for the
price of a good pair of walking shoes which everyone
should wear anyway. What walking calls for is the simple
determination to do it. This most people lack! That is why
this chapter has been included in this book.

It has been well said that many of the most precious
things in life are absolutely free. Walking is one of them.
It can begin at your own front door.

   Go out and claim the clouds without cost.
      Stir your spirit with the splendor of sunset and
        sunrise.
         Lift up your eyes to the hills and renew your
           strength.
            Inhale the perfume of flowers, trees and shrubs
              heavy in the air.
      Widen your horizons with wide vistas over lakes
        and fields.
      Stand silent before sun, moon, and starry skies.

Be still and know that God is here.

Far too many people have been deceived into believing that God can only be found in the sanctuary of a church; in the speaking of sermons; in some high-powered evangelistic program; in some difficult doctrinal discourse.

Yet, all around us in the natural realm which He has created, Christ speaks to us clearly. The heavens actually do proclaim the very character of God. The wonders of the earth do disclose His handiwork. Our problem is we are not prepared to give Him either the respect of our attention or the benefit of our time.

We are too preoccupied with our own pet priorities.

We prefer to pander to our own self-interests.

It seems absurd just to *"Walk with God literally"* in gentle humility.

The ancient prophet Micah put it very plainly!

"He (the Almighty One) hath shewed you, O man,
what is good; and what doth the Lord require of you,
but to do justly (be fair), and to love mercy,
and to walk humbly with your God!?" (Micah 6:8).

This practice of getting outdoors and getting alone with our Father for an intimate interlude is either too simple, too practical or perhaps a bit too frightening for most people. Most of my contemporaries prefer the polished programs of the church where, they are convinced, one is much more certain to commune with Christ.

Those few brave enough to walk humbly with Him in the quietness of the hills or along the banks of a lake or stream will be surprised at the pure pleasure of His presence with them. They will discover how He does divert their attention by the fragrance of the flowers; the serene songs of the birds, the winds, the waters; the quiet beauty of the earth, sky and clouds.

In such moments of tranquility I turn quietly to Him and give humble, genuine gratitude for so much beauty. A profound renewal of spirit takes place within me. My soul is quickened, enlivened and strengthened by the glory and wonder of His handiwork all around me. A serene sense of peace and repose replaces the fret and rub of life. All is well within.

Any one of us common people can own the wonder and grandeur of the earth. They are free for the taking. But it does take time to possess them in personal encounter. I need not be a millionaire who owns great country properties to be rich in the bounties of my God. He gives us freely, without price, all things to enjoy. Every gracious benefit comes to me as a generous gift from my Father—*if I will accept it!*

So it is essential that I must go outdoors in a joyous, carefree attitude of happy adventure. I must expect some lovely surprises. This is plain, old-fashioned faith in action. And by the time I return from my ramble I shall be richer in lovely memories and more robust in health than when I left.

This is the atmosphere which envelopes me when I pull on my well worn walking shoes; slip into a comfortable outdoor jacket; then head out in high spirits. It is all part and parcel of a wholesome life, a healthy outlook and a soul made strong in company with Christ.

There are abounding other benefits which come to the person who learns to love the out-of-doors. Excellent physical exercise to tone up the body; the stimulation of fresh air, sunshine and broader horizons for the mind. Each in their own way enrich the day and energize our lives. The truly astonishing thing is how few find these treasures just outside their doors.

Little by little, it seems, there is a growing interest among the general public in outdoor activities. This is encouraging, because as more people find pleasure and renewal in the natural world they will learn to cherish and preserve this outdoor environment. And certainly God's people need to be alert and awake to their part in preserving our priceless heritage.

In the early stages of the conservation cause, brave Christians like John Muir, Jack Miner and Theodore Roosevelt were bold to speak out on behalf of the natural wonders of the earth. They called for reverence and respect for the natural resources with which God our Father has endowed us. We should do the same. Not just for the sake of endangered species and a threatened environment, but also for the well being of our own species.

The splendor and glory of the earth can inspire us. As God's children we must learn to claim this wondrous heritage without diminishing its beauty—or its vitality!

15

NOURISHING THE SOUL

If one is to be strong physically the body must be nourished consistently with wholesome, nutritious food. In precisely the same way if any person is to be strong in soul and spirit they must be nourished consistently with spiritual truth and principles.

A spiritual diet that consists of no more than a couple of church services a week will produce a Christian who is weak, vulnerable to the invasion of destructive ideas and damaging world concepts. When Christ included the phrase, *"Give us this day our daily bread,"* in His prayer it referred to more than bread and butter. He also had food for the soul in mind.

It requires a great deal of careful thought, daily effort, time, planning and loving preparation to nourish our bodies properly. So much so that food is one of the favorite pastimes in which people participate. It is also one of the favorite topics which they love to discuss.

By the same sort of measurement many Christians

have virtually no interest in spending their time or thought or money on nourishing their souls. Without wincing they will gladly spend $20.00 on a fancy dinner out for two, several times a month. But they feel $20.00 is an outrageous price to pay for a good book that could change the whole course of their communion with Christ for twenty years. The dinner is over and done with in two hours. The well-read book can impact their lives for eternity, as well as that of others to whom they might lend it.

This commonplace comparison is given here to show how people perceive the importance of nourishing their souls. Good devotional books or inspirational works are by no means the only source of splendid nutrition for the soul. But they, along with God's Word, can combine to strengthen and sustain any soul who studies them, ruminates in them and assimilates their truths.

Looking back over my own life I here declare without apology that it is the study of God's Word year after year, close communion with Christ, and great books that have nourished my soul in wondrous ways. Such authors as Fenelon, Henry Drummond, F. B. Meyer, G. Campbell Morgan, Martyn Lloyd Jones, A. W. Tozer, Hannah Whitehall Smith, Oswald Chambers, Andrew Murray and John Stott have each, with their own special insights, enriched my life beyond measure.

The profound principles they have learned to live by daily and passed on to me through their wholesome work have been a tremendous source of strength to my soul and uplift to my spirit. In sincerity and genuine gratitude I give God my Father thanks daily for beautiful books, the same as for the home-baked bread Ursula turns out with such skill and love.

Just last week I stumbled across a small, somewhat inconspicuous little paperback copy of a book I had purchased in 1967 (25 years ago). I had started to study it then, but somehow, during the drastic days of my first wife's death, it had been misplaced, only to be discovered again last week. It is so dry, so brittle with age, so broken backed that each page I turn tears loose from the spine. Yet on each precious page there are flashes of divine illumination and profound, stirring principles of eternal truth such as I have not read for years and years.

The work was first written and published exactly 100 years ago. Yet today, lying open, broken, and eagerly read on my desk it has nourished my soul with food from above. It is as though I am a private guest who has come to a royal banquet, to relish the finest fare my Father could provide. It is not just a case of being stirred in spirit by the beautiful insights of this saint of God. Much, much more than that is the sustenance and strength of soul that is mine from communing with Christ through the truths revealed.

The time has come, in the history of the church, to remind God's people that their souls will starve if they are not nourished by the bounties of God's own Word and the blessings of great and noble books. A royal tradition of lofty, inspiring literature has been left to this generation. But most Christians have not even tasted the wondrous truths and fine fare available to them.

Just as with our bodies, so also with our souls, we are what we eat. If we consume only sugars and sweets along with junk food we will, in a literal sense, become "junkies." And if we consume only the deceptive entertainment of the world and feed our minds and emotions on the trash turned out by the media we will become ignorant people devoid of spiritual strength or discernment.

One of God's great giants penned these lines in the last century. Contemporary Christians need to heed them!

"If we will take the Word of God, His revealed truth, into our lips and eat it, that is, if we will dwell upon His words and say them over and over to ourselves, then we shall take them in and assimilate their meaning. In this common sense way we shall find that our soul is fed and nourished by them. So we are made strong and vigorous. . . ."

To which we must then add the simple, instant action of carrying out Christ's commands in quiet but implicit obedience. This is the responsible conduct of a child of God who exercises forthright faith in God.

This is the person who comes to have complete confidence in the counsel and guidance of the Gracious Holy Spirit.

In all this there is strength of soul and serenity of spirit.

There is a profound principle at work here which is neglected by most people. The things which we think about and meditate over in our minds feed our souls. But even more important it is our inner thoughts which shape our characters, control our conduct and direct our conversation.

Of course most people make an effort to be *"civilized."* There is a veneer of respectability which is drawn over what they discuss in public or how they behave among believers. Yet beneath the surface their thought-life may be vile and repulsive, conditioned by our crass and corrupt culture.

In our contemporary society all sorts of perverse ideas and deceptive values are propagated in public. The base ideas of unbelievers, the subtle suggestions of sensualists, the gross cynicism of agnostics, the empty philosophies of humanism abound all around us. They are in our newspapers, in our magazines, in our television programs, in our radio broadcasts, in our book stores, in our class rooms, in our colleges, in our industry, government and social life. No wonder we are a world gone wrong!

The only viable antidote for all the degradation around us is the indwelling power and presence of Christ Himself. He and only He can so sustain and energize our souls by His Word, His life, His Spirit, His truth that we can turn our backs on the world and walk in His Way. This means we must meditate and muse over His Word, His life, His work. We must saturate our minds, our emotions, our wills in His truth, His teaching, His temper. His thoughts thus become our thoughts and we become energized by His Mind.

Then, and only then, can we begin to think on those things which are noble, honest, beautiful, pure and eternal. This is the secret to purity of spirit, honesty of motive and power to prevail with God and man in a mad world.

It may be helpful here to suggest several simple ways which can make the study and reading of God's Word rewarding and uplifting. Many people have often asked me how to do it.

First of all find a quiet spot where you can be alone, undisturbed and very still in Christ's presence. Provide yourself with a good light, a table to write at, and a private notebook kept only for your use . . . plus a good pen that writes well.

Come to this rendezvous with God, wide awake,

washed and fully alert, prepared to be attentive to God's Spirit. A profound inner attitude of respect and anticipation is essential.

Bring your favorite Bible, as well as at least one other translation in a modern idiom. And do not hesitate to mark them freely. A concordance can be helpful.

Before beginning to read, bow your spirit before Christ in humility and reverence. Quiet your mind and emotions in His presence. Allow His serenity to sweep into your soul. Then in sincerity ask Him to speak clearly to you through the passage you are reading for the day.

It is best to work your way gently and carefully through an entire gospel, epistle, or book. Do not hop, skip and jump around at random. Each sentence, each statement, each clear command that comes to your attention should be written down in your notebook in your own words in ordinary language you understand. Ask God's Holy Spirit to guide you.

Compare scripture with scripture on that theme. Get to know all that God's Word reveals about that subject. Thank your Father for showing you plainly what His purposes and promises are for you as His child. Then *write down your determination* to carry them out in your daily conduct with faith in His help to do so.

Within three months your soul will be strengthened mightily!

The same sort of procedure helps in reading and poring over any devotional or inspirational book. Read and re-read them. Mark them, make notes in the margins, ruminate over what has been written. Give God your time, your serious thought, your single-minded attention so you can actually respond to what He is saying to you.

In this way certain books, specific chapters, and important themes will become a treasure trove to you. You will soon become a person of deep convictions, of great loyalty to Christ—one who knows Him, loves Him, serves Him, trusts Him, obeys Him and draws others to Him.

The soul food you derive from God's Word will so nourish and sustain and strengthen your soul, you will never again be satisfied with the pabulum served from so many pulpits. You will have learned to hear from Christ Himself, and in that acute awareness His Word will become to you spirit and life. It will energize you, thrill you and empower you to accomplish much in His honor.

In the same way it is surprising how our thoughts, ideas, convictions and values are shaped by those people with whom we associate. Too many times we allow the people with a worldly mind set to influence us. Especially if we see them often, work with them or spend our leisure time together. Even if they are pleasant, gracious individuals but with no knowledge of Christ or His Way, they can readily weaken the witness we have within of God's Gracious Spirit.

So I urge the reader to make a point of picking strong and stalwart Christians as your companions. Spend time with those who in sincerity walk humbly with the Lord. Cultivate the company of those who enjoy His Presence and find great joy in giving Him honor and gratitude for His part in their lives. Their delight will strengthen your soul.

Allow me to say again, in all earnestness, that a couple of casual church services a week, with perhaps an odd prayer meeting thrown in, if convenient, will not suffice to nourish your soul or strengthen your spirit in God. You do not try to get by on three meals a week for your bodily well-being. How then can one hope to be spiritually strong on such a spartan diet?

The matter has been discussed elsewhere in this book, but it is so important that I touch on it here once more as a means of strengthening your soul in God, our Father. It really is a sublime spiritual secret, exercised by so few.

Do just take time to commune with Christ Himself. Do converse with Him privately, but audibly and honestly, about every aspect of your life. Allow Him openly and freely to enter every area of your daily experiences—your home, your family, your business, your travel, your pastimes, your money, your investments, your leisure. Seek wisdom, insight, direction from Him in *all* your decisions. As He is given control of your affairs a tremendous sense of inner well-being, and supernatural (His) strength, will pervade your soul. You will become a powerful person with a potent purpose to your life. And it will be the very life of the Risen Christ in you who impacts your generation.

All of the foregoing is sometimes called the prayer of faith.

Alongside continuous communion with Christ, there must be a constant expression of humble thanks and genuine gratitude to our Father for every part He plays in your loving association. Make the deliberate effort to remember every beautiful benefit as well as every loving discipline He bestows. Thank Him aloud. Thank Him sincerely. Thank Him often. Thank Him with genuine joy in the presence of others so they too are aware of His faithfulness.

This is what is sometimes called the praise of the spirit.

It will uplift and enrich your soul. Most important it pleases Him.

16

MAKING MUSIC

Music in all of its diverse forms is one of the greatest gifts which God our Father has bestowed upon the planet and its people. Music is an essential aspect of the very character of God Himself. Even before the creation of the earth the stars in their galaxies sang together in joyous celebration of the might and power of The Most High. All His wondrous works were formed in the most exquisite harmony and were intended to function with glorious joy and thrilling melodies.

Wherever God moves and works and resides there is the majestic music of the eternal presence of His person. He always has been "The Master Music Maker"; "The Supreme Composer of all Melodic Compositions"; "The Divine Creator of all Comfort and Consolation."

In a word Christ Himself is the Lord of all joy! He is The Instigator of the music which moves across the ages and moves across our human heart strings—to use an old and well-worn phrase. His earnest will and highest hope for us bungling human beings is that through His love, grace, compassion and forgiveness we might be brought into true harmony with Him.

From the earliest days of creation He created harmony. Far and wide across the great expanses of the earth He brought magnificent melodies into play. The songs of the sea; the lilting melodies of running streams; the whispering notes of the wind in the trees; the glorious sounds of a thousand bird songs; the muted stirrings of breezes blowing over fields of grass and grain; the lovely lap of water on the lake edge; the sweet sounds of rain falling from the clouds; the gentle murmur of contented children at play; the deep chuckle of adults sweet in spirit; the glorious songs of lives spilling over with abundant joy.

He made them all! And He invites us to make music too with our little lives.

Put in the plainest possible language, He urges us to be joyful—to be filled with joy—to be joyous individuals. Joy, His joy, should be our joy. This quality of good will, of good cheer, of merriment, melodies and mirth should be the music of our souls. We are to be people of sweet singing spirits, of harmonious will in harmony with His will, and of deep delight. He loves to hear us make music that endures for eternity. He longs to share in the sweet songs of serenity that spring up from our souls when we are contented in His company. He actually lives with the person who pours out melodies of praise from a truly penitent and pure personality which has found peace and joy with Him.

As a small lad, perhaps the most powerful impact made on my life by my mother was the music she made. Though she was a stern teacher, she was also a glorious

music-maker around our home. She had been richly endowed with one of the most magnificent soprano voices I
ever heard. Not only was it an instrument of great purity
but also of remarkable range and power. She had never
taken formal training. But that did not deter her from
bursting into song at any moment either in the privacy of
her home or in public gatherings.

I recall vividly how during the discouraging and very
difficult days when I was a small child and she and Dad
were locked in a stern struggle with the primitive forces of
evil among the pagan people all around us, her singing
was such a source of strength for all of us. She would
spend hours and hours on her knees crying out to Christ
for the redemption of perishing people living in the huts
across our hills. Then in triumph of spirit she would start
to sing thrilling, stirring songs of praise and triumph that
rose to a great crescendo across the countryside. The
Africans listened in awe!

In services, I saw her lead thousands of jubilant Africans, who also love to sing, in glorious harmony without
the benefit or aid of any public address system. Her voice
would soar in splendor encouraging the whole congrega-
tion to join in jubilant praise and awesome adoration.
God, by His Spirit, had moved mightily among the people,
and in part it was because of her prayers and in part
because of her magnificent music making. In deed and in
truth there had been an exchange of beauty for ashes and
the garment of joyous praise for the spirit of heaviness.

Of course, not all of us are gifted with a golden voice
like my mother was. Nor do some of us even have the
capacity to carry a tune for more than twenty notes. We
cannot even play an instrument, much less make the sort

of music generally associated with pleasant sounds or moving melodies. If we do we are fortunate and uniquely endowed.

Yet each of us needs to make music. And the music that I am referring to in this chapter is that of the soul and of the spirit. It has its source in the realm of the supernatural. It emerges from the remarkable ability of our Father to take any one of us and employ our own unique personality and character as an instrument of music in His hands. He the Christ, the Master Composer, can draw from us harmonies, melodies and songs of delight that bring Him enormous joy and satisfaction. Besides that, the music of our lives can be pure pleasure to others.

Here is the sort of soul music that I speak of here. It is a short refrain drawn from a letter to us this week. . . .

"How nice it was for you to put up with us again!
I always feel loved, blessed and renewed when
I leave your place. I can't thank you enough
for just being there, when we needed you!"

That is the music of gratitude and good will.

In the contemporary language of our day, much is made of the phrase, *"quality of life."* It is a catch-all phrase, that refers in an obscure way to living life at a higher level than most people experience. It has a vague connotation that somehow it is possible to add a rare spiritual dimension to our earthly sojourn. In fact, some people call it almost a "fad," particularly for young people, many of whom have grown up in an environment, both at home; in school; and in the world as a whole, where God our Father is unknown and Christ is a stranger.

The supreme secret to the highest quality of life is to know The Eternal Father first hand . . . and *to know Him as my Father; and to know the living Christ as my dearest Friend and Majesty; and to know His Gracious Holy Spirit as my closest Counselor.*

In this magnificent relationship there is intense joy and rest. This is the supreme song of the soul set free from self-preoccupation, from selfish self-interest, from all the vanity of self-satisfaction.

The center of our exultation is now found in the character of Christ. The joy of our days is generated in the essential goodness, grace and generosity of God, our Father. Our harmony arises from the well-spring of His presence and His peace within by His Holy Spirit.

This is what it means to "rejoice in the Lord"—not just in His benefits and blessings bestowed on us every day, but in the wonder and exuberance of His profound Person. He touches and transforms me and all that pertains to me at a thousand points in life. It is He who gives me His eternal life, His supernatural life, His superb quality of life, His abundant life.

This joy, this ecstasy, this assurance is the music of my soul, the song of my spirit, the strength of my life.

It endures because He endures. It is eternal because He is eternal. *This is the music of the Master.*

In all the world there is no greater magnet to attract men and women to our Savior than the song of the soul set free. It is the magnificent music of the Most High. Its melodies are of divine arrangement and its harmonies come from Christ the Master Composer.

Believers can proclaim their beliefs; devout Christians can contend for their doctrines; scholars can argue their academic differences, yet not one will so quickly move the soul of a perishing person as the joyous music of a simple man whose song of delight is God Himself. It is Christ's way of calling others to Himself.

Show me the person whose life reverberates with the music of the Master and I will show you a supreme soul-winner—a term not well understood by Christians highly programmed by their churches. So many are sure they must use special techniques.

Yesterday morning early I went for a quiet walk along our country road. A car pulled off to park in an area where there were no houses. Out jumped a beautiful big German Shepherd, followed a few moments later by a wiry, little old man, tough as a pair of cowboy chaps.

A deep, powerful urge within constrained me to cross the road and chat with this crusty character—a total stranger. In less than six sentences a stream of anger and profanity poured from his lips. He hated the highway department for changing the road. He swore at *"big business"* for busting up the country. He cursed out the telephone people for tapping his line. He poured out abuse on all the rotten politicians who pocketed his tax dollars.

When his diatribe was done, and his spleen was spent, I simply smiled at him gently and remarked, "You really can't trust any of them, can you? But there is One you can trust completely. Christ will never doublecross you. God, our Father, is absolutely faithful to anyone who comes to Him!"

His jaw dropped. His eyes took on a misty haze. He gazed straight into my face and spoke softly.

"Sir, forgive my awful profanity. You see, I really am searching for God. I know I must meet Him on judgment day!" He looked at me with enormous pathos in his eyes. His handsome dog came over to console him, and sniff my legs.

I looked in his old car. There on the passenger seat lay an open Bible he had been reading but not understanding. Quietly I invited this total stranger to simply put his implicit trust in Christ—the One who could give him beauty for his ashes of anger; praise in place of all his vile profanity; music of soul instead of awful cynicism.

Jubilant with joy he shouted to me as I walked away, "He is King of Kings! He will reign forever! He never changes! I will be in church this Sunday morning!"

Are you surprised that a sublime song arose in my own soul as I rambled down the road, headed for home? This is music making for the common man on the common road.

Without shame, without apology, without embarrassment we can calmly share our confidence in Christ with others. It is not something stiff, starchy or stilted. It is the transparent joy of knowing our Father first hand and gently introducing others to Him in eager expectancy.

The ancient and revered Psalmist, David, put these concepts—this "quality of life"—into these poetic phrases. They are pure music.

> *"Thou (O God) will show me the path of life:*
> *In Thy presence is fullness of joy:*
> *At Thy right hand there are pleasures for evermore!"*
> Psalm 16:11

Those refrains ring true!
They are the harmony of heaven on earth!
This is the music of an abundant life in Christ!

His life brings laughter to our lips. It generates great good will within. It creates wondrous good cheer amid our adversity. It resonates with harmony in the heart. His life empowers us to overcome all obstacles hour by hour. This is true strength of soul, sweet serenity of spirit.

Hannah Whitall Smith, that remarkable lady who truly loved Christ is such a simple, shining way, wrote these lines about her dad, "I remember my dear father who was a saint on earth, if ever there was one, but, I must confess, a very jolly one, teaching me a great lesson. A friend had reproved him for laughing merrily on a solemn occasion. He turned to me and said in his merry voice, calling me by my pet name, '*Han, if people who know their sins are forgiven, and that God loves them and cares for them cannot laugh, I don't know who can!*'"

There it is, the making of music from the soul.

This is a quality of life which injects enormous pleasure into our pilgrimage. It bursts out in song, and laughter, and lightheartedness with the spontaneity of a mountain spring. It drives away despair and dispels discouragement. It soothes the soul, energizes the spirit and heals our bodies—if we will let Him into every area of life.

Allow me to emphasize that the merry heart that makes music for the Master is not intended to enrich and restore only my own soul. It is also intended by our Father to be the sweet sound and magnificent melody that He can use to draw others to Himself. In this He employs our melodies to lift loads, heal hurts and bring good cheer to the weary ones all around us.

My music making can set others to singing.
   It can be a balm of blessing to my generation.
      God's people can supply songs amid the world's sadness.
      In so doing we also delight our Father no end.

What an honor!

17

MEMORIALS OF HONOR

With the adventure of life common to all of us, the part played by memory becomes increasingly important. We make all sorts of jokes about failing memory. We excuse eccentric behavior because of unreliable power of recall. We learn to laugh at our own lapses of mind. Some go so far as to take special courses in ways to sharpen and enhance this capacity.

My favorite comment in this connection is, "I have a marvelous memory. But it is very short."

Putting all pleasantries aside, there remains the vital question, *"What can be done in honor with my memory?"* For it is an aspect of our lives that deserves greater respect than just being turned into a joke. In actual fact memory is a remarkable capacity given to us by God our Father for noble purposes. Without it we could not even learn. With its wise use our lives can be enriched with remarkable treasures deposited in our memory bank, then withdrawn on demand, to be re-lived and relished again.

It is this aspect which finds its most poignant expression in what we usually call *"storytelling."* In ancient time, before the common use of written language, the traditions of the tribe and the wisdom of the wise were all transmitted from generation to generation by storytelling. In most primitive societies the gathering of the family or friends or clan around the evening fire was the most memorable part of the entire day. That was storytelling time!

Through the age-old process of recounting folk lore and folk tales parents and elders passed on their experiences and accumulated insights to their children. It was a highly esteemed, honorable exercise whereby the family and society prospered and flourished. Storytelling was a joyous activity, and the able storyteller was highly respected in society.

I grew up in a period of time, amid primitive people, for whom storytelling was a precious and poignant part of life. I picked up the skills and joys of storytelling from my African companions at an early age. Even later in life I shared hundreds of evening campfires with congenial friends, or family, where we sat beneath the stars and poured out our treasure trove of precious memories to each other.

So it is not surprising that across the years, many have come to call me *"the storyteller."* It is a title which I am not ashamed to bear. For it has been my aim to use this joyous gift not only to bring pleasure to my hearers, but also genuine honor to God, my Father.

It is this last point to which this chapter is devoted. For I am acutely aware that in our so-called *"sophisticated society,"* the role of thestory teller has diminished almost to extinction. In its place have come libraries of cheap paperback books; the tyranny of television; and the computer memory bank. At the push of a button our minds are exposed to whatever was pre-programmed. All of us are poorer for it.

So what I am here pleading for is a return to the art of recounting the memorable events in our lives which were designed and arranged in the loving care of our Father. Some of my readers will shrug this off with the caustic remark, "So what?" But I have lived long enough to know that the person who is prepared, in humility, and in sincerity, to share the spiritual experiences of his or her own walk with Christ brings honor to Him and benefit to others.

It is not an easy thing to do for it calls for self-exposure. Most people prefer to draw a screen of privacy around their lives. Yet strange to say God Himself delights to have us declare what He has achieved on our behalf.

The recounting of His part and place in our little lives can bring Him great honor. It also strengthens our own souls.

In reading the Gospel accounts of our Lord's life on earth, it always impressed me deeply how Christ commanded those whom He had touched or healed to go home and tell their friends and families. From His perspective it was essential to recount the encounter . . . in detail!

Why? Why not just keep it very personal, very private? As so many people often say to me, "After all, my religion is a very personal thing! It is a private decision what I choose to believe!"

To a point that is true. But if the "personal thing" is a

personal encounter with the Living Christ, the impact on the life, the character and conduct is such that one cannot long remain silent. Others will know at once you have met the Master. They will be aware you have been with Him. And if they hunger and thirst for truth they will ask you to tell them the story of your own walk with Him.

Across the past thirty years of my life it has astonished me again and again to have people ask me in the utmost earnestness, "How did you come to know Christ?" or "Why is God so real to you, and not to me?"

So the questions go on and on, and so the opportunities go on, to tell the story of my Father's wondrous concern and compassion for one so wayward and willful. I am not ashamed to share with others the incredible generosity and amazing grace of Christ in forgiving me, accepting me, remaking me. It is a thrilling story of the transforming power of His Presence; the dynamic of His own dear Spirit; the invincibility of His Word.

These living encounters with the Living God cannot be faked. They are the marvelous memories of magnificent moments in company with Christ. And without apology they are retold in awe and wonder. They are memorials to His love, His faithfulness, His might.

They remain and they endure because they are true to Him.

Just last evening a friend and I took a short stroll down to the lake edge. It had been a ferociously hot, humid day, so the cool fresh breeze blowing off the water was a splendid refreshment. We sat beneath a gnarled old pine and listened to the soft lap of the waves on the shore.

As we relaxed in each other's company I was thrilled

and refreshed by another gentle breeze. For the wind of God's Gracious Spirit stirred our souls as we recounted to each other the remarkable faithfulness of our Father in caring for each of us across the long years of our lives. We were sharing our memories of how generous, how gracious, how gentle God had been to provide and protect us in every situation.

He had been a mission pilot in Canada's far north for 33 years. Amid the ice, the snow, the blizzards, the cruel, long, dark winters he and his family had served the frontier people of that tough territory without flinching—all because of strength of soul and serenity of spirit which came from Christ.

We were like two lads, laughing and joking together in great good humor, chuckling with pure joy and enormous delight over the goodness of our Father. It was not a case of boasting or bragging about our adventures in adversity. Rather, it was the pure pleasure of telling how we could trust in God and find Him utterly reliable in every aspect of our lives.

Mirth and contentment and faith and loyalty to Christ flowed between us in joyous exultation. We were invigorated in spirit, strengthened in soul and vitalized in body. More than that I am sure the angels sang and our Father smiled upon us in pleasure. We walked home in the gathering twilight refreshed and renewed.

Ever since I came to North America as a teenage lad, it has impressed me profoundly to observe, first hand, how hard it seems for Christians here to converse about Christ. They seem almost embarrassed to even mention His name outside the stilted setting of the church sanctuary. Seldom if ever do they speak joyously, spontaneously, intimately about God as their loving Father. Much more often they simply refer to Him vaguely and obliquely as *"the Lord"* or *"the good Lord"* or *"the One upstairs"* as if they only had a rather remote and nodding acquaintance with Him.

Again and again I have tried to turn a conversation toward the joy and inspiration and adventure of sharing life with Christ and having Him share life with us. A strange silence descends upon the room. People become uneasy. There is an acute embarrassment that we are discussing a dimension of life unfamiliar and unreal. They would much rather talk about the baseball series; the newest pizza parlor in town; the last trip to Hawaii; or the next political election.

The prevailing impression one gets is that somehow we are to keep our religion very private, very personal, very much buttoned up in our shirt pockets. But in contrast the Word, the command, that comes to us clearly is, *"Let the redeemed of the Lord say so!!"* And this does not mean in just some strident, sanctimonious way in a sanctuary.

The time has come in our history as a civilization, that the people of God must be bold enough, brave enough and big hearted enough to speak gladly to anyone about God, their Father and Christ their Friend. If they have not yet come to know Him that well, then it is high time they did. Nothing is so potent in impacting another person for Christ as the sincere, unashamed life and language of one who truly knows and loves Him.

It is a contagion! It is genuine! It honors our Father!

If one reads God's Word with care, it is astonishing to discover two tremendous lines of thought running through the revelation. They run parallel to each other and provide clear direction to us in the matter of how to use our memories in order to honor God and at the same time enrich others while strengthening our own souls.

The first powerful principle is to actually report and record the remarkable relationship between God and man. Large segments of the Scriptures are a detailed account of how human beings responded to the person and presence of the Most High. There is an unvarnished story told of how He was willing to enter their lives, guide their decisions, provide for their needs and deliver them from adversity.

In short, the history of God dealing with people is in fact also *His story* of His enduring faithfulness to us fallible, fickle human beings. Again and again the Lord God commands that these events be recorded and repeated for the benefit and instruction of following generations. It was to be an enduring memorial to His honor and integrity!

The second clear command given to us scores of times is that we should recount these events continually. We should be bold enough on our Father's behalf to tell others of His wondrous character, His intense compassion, His intimate care, His loving provision for us.

How else is a cynical society, so contemptuous of Christ, ever to realize how real He is; how dear He is; how near He is to those who follow Him in calm confidence? It is we who must tell the glad story of His unfailing goodness.

This should be done not only verbally but also in writing. It increases our faith in Christ actually to sit down in private and put on paper the pulsing, living, dynamic interaction of our little lives with God Himself. How few ever take the time to do this!

Is it not strange that we write notes of thanks and send letters of appreciation to people who have shown us kindness? Yet we seem to think it is absurd, or even childish, to extend the same sort of courtesy to our Father. Are we so tough-minded and hard-hearted (stubborn), that we refuse to record all the beautiful bonuses He bestows upon us in such abundance? Or to show our love for Christ in this simple way?

If so, then it implies we take such benefits for granted. Like the worldlings all around us we assume we just have them coming to us. So our attitude is one of carnal indifference.

Show me the person who takes the time and thought and sensitivity to express genuine esteem for God's generosity daily, and I will show you a person with steel in his or her soul. You will find such an individual has intimate interaction with Christ continuously. Out of this personal profound pattern of giving praise to the Most High comes strength of character and superb serenity of spirit.

What I have described in this chapter is not a fairy tale. It is not some vague sort of fanciful piety that a few religious recluses practice. It is the daily discipline of a soul that loves God and is loyal to Him with deep devotion.

When a young man and young woman—or an older man and older woman—fall in love with each other what happens? Every other consideration in life is set aside. They make time to be together. They spend hours speaking to each other. They find special pleasure in writing notes and letters of affection. They tell others gladly of their beloved. If we can do all of this so readily for another human being, then surely, surely, we can do the same for our Beloved One, our Living Christ . . . and God our Father.

Perhaps, like so many things in our life with Him, it is too simple, too ordinary, too commonplace. So we just skip it. *Try it and see what happens!*

18

NO DEBTS, NO DESPAIR

The title of this chapter may suggest to the reader that its main theme is money and financial matters. Not so, except in part, as it touches briefly upon our responsibility to honor God with our income.

There is a much wider area of discharging our debts of obligation in the realm of our personal relationships to God and man. These debts are not often discussed in the way in which they will be here. For most people have not understood what debt does to us.

Debt of any kind is actually a drag on life. It is something which is owed to another. It puts us under pressure until it is repaid. It oppresses us as an obligation which must be discharged. Debt can lead to despair and discouragement. It can dominate our days, determine our decisions, and, if not dealt with properly, lead to destruction. In financial terms this is called bankruptcy. Likewise there can be moral and spiritual bankruptcy.

We incur debt by our own decisions. At some point in time, usually under duress, we take on obligations that later must be discharged. And if we delay or default on the repayment we become bogged down deeper and deeper in debt. The end result is deeper distress.

In His mercy and compassion for us the Spirit of God instructs us clearly not to incur debts. Here is what He says:

"Keep out of debt altogether, except that perpetual debt of love which we owe one another, for he that loveth another hath followed the law" (Romans 13:8).

This is a divine law, a spiritual principle, for strength of soul and serenity of spirit. It is the key to contentment, a way to well being.

Because I have dealt with the matter of financial debt in a forceful way in other books, especially in *God Is My Delight*, I do not propose to go over that ground here again. But I do have a serious responsibility to warn the reader that continuing to carry a debt load could lead to your financial ruin in the near future. The world-wide economic malaise that comes from so much debt may well destroy all the financial institutions which men and nations have held in such high esteem. It has happened before. It can happen again!

God's person should be free of debt. There is an enormous buoyancy of spirit and stability of mind in the individual who has no burdensome financial obligations. They are strong souls who can honor our Father with generous giving of tithes and offerings. They are also the sturdy ones who are strong enough to reach out and help the poor, the underprivileged, the truly perishing people of society.

I am not here referring to some sort of proud paternalism. Nor am I speaking of impressive philantrophic activities. I have in mind the simple, humble compassion of caring for others in need. It is owning a warm heart and open hand that shares gladly with those who struggle to survive. Each of us can do it. And the world will be better for it.

Now I wish to deal with the other forms of debt which are just as deadly, just as difficult as those that involve money. They are of enormous importance in life between us and God, and us and others, as well as with ourselves.

Let me illustrate what I mean through common phrases we use. For example:

"I owe him an apology!"
"We owe them a visit."
"I owe her a letter."
"We owe ourselves a vacation."
"I owe God more of my time."
"I owe so much to my friend."

These are all debts not discharged. They lead to despair and ennui. Jesus, the Christ, was acutely aware of them too. So much so that they are a prominent part of the great prayer He gave us:

"And forgive us our debts, as we forgive our debtors!"
Matthew 6:12.

Dr. J. B. Phillips put it this way in his fine translation:

"Forgive us what we owe to you (O God our Father) as we have also forgiven those who owe anything to us!"

Christ enlarged on this matter of debt by emphasizing at once, "For if you forgive other people their failures, your Heavenly Father will also forgive you. But if you will not forgive other people, neither will your Heavenly Father forgive you your failures (debts)."

So debts are tremendously important to tranquility in life. How they are discharged and how they are dealt with, each day, in large measure determine the health of soul and joy of spirit we own.

Because I am a very practical person who attempts to deal with the complexities of life in a simple, straightforward manner I here make some serious suggestions. If you owe someone an apology, go to them at once and make things right in sincerity. If you owe someone a visit, set aside your own schedule and go for the visit in good will. If you owe a letter, turn off the wretched T.V., pick up a pen and write the letter with hope and encouragement in its lines. You will feel better for it. If you are wearing out from overwork and owe yourself a rest, drop everything and take a break. Get outside your same four walls, even if you can only afford to take a joyous, lighthearted walk in the open countryside. I do this often with delight. If you owe God more of your time and attention, for your own sake as well as His, get up half an hour earlier and give Him the best time of your day—the dawn. If you owe a friend deep gratitude for help and love, don't delay, tell him or her so.

Tell them often. Tell them without embarrassment. Enrich their lives!

Ninety percent of genuine Christianity lies in our will.

Either—with Christ's presence and power—we set our wills to discharge our debts and do His will, or we drift like a dying fish in a stream of despair.

Either we are people with steel in our spines who determine with His grace to carry out our Father's will, or we are pathetic, weak-kneed procrastinators who just prefer to loaf and do nothing for God or man. Then we get deeper and deeper in debt with the darkness of despair surrounding our souls.

Allow Christ to control your life. Let Him live and move and have His way in you. It is possible for you to will and to do of His good pleasure. Then you will be on top of things. And your life can be a triumph—not a torment!

What I am saying is we need to keep short accounts with God and man. We need to have our debts discharged. Often they are much greater than we ever imagine or realize. The following letter, composed by someone unknown to me, puts our position in an unforgettable, heart-stopping way, from Christ's perspective.

Dear Friend,

I just had to send a note to tell you how much I love you and care about you. I saw you yesterday as you were walking with your friends. I waited all day hoping you would want to talk to me also. As evening drew near, I gave you a sunset to close your day and a cool breeze to rest you. And I waited. But you never came. It hurt me, but I still love you because I am your friend.

I saw you fall asleep last night and I longed to touch your brow. So, I spilled moonlight on your pillow and your face. Again I waited, wanting to rush down so that we could talk. I have so many gifts for you. But you awakened late the next day and rushed off to work. My tears were in the rain.

Today you looked so sad, so all alone. It makes my heart ache because I understand. My friends let me down and hurt me so many times, too. But I love you. Oh, if you would only listen to me. I really love you. I try to tell you in the blue sky and in quiet green grass. I whisper it in the leaves on the trees and breathe it in the colors of the flowers. I shout it to you in the mountain streams and give the birds love songs to sing. I clothe you with warm sunshine and perfume the air with nature's scents. My love for you is deeper than the oceans and bigger than the biggest want or need in your heart.

If you only knew how much I want to help you. I want you to meet my Father. He wants to help you, too. My Father is that way, you know. Just call me, ask me, talk with me. I have so much to share with you.

But I won't hassle you. I'll wait because I love you.

Your friend,
Jesus the Christ.

In our daily interaction with Christ and with other people, as this dramatic little letter makes clear, we do incur debts. To help the reader understand better I shall list some of those which seem to injure us most.

The debt of common courtesy for each other.
The debt of promises made but never fulfilled.
The debt of cheerful encouragement in adversity, withheld.
The debt of insensitivity for those who suffer.

The debt of neglect for one another in loneliness.
The debt of just not caring about others.
The debt of silence, when praise is needed.

As those who claim to be children of our Father, we cannot in integrity say we belong to Him, yet behave like this. It is a contradiction in terms. It is what brings so much contempt upon Christians. It needs serious correction. And the only One who can achieve this correction in our characters and in our conduct is Christ Himself. It is He who can change us by the drastic, inner re-creation of His own person, His own power, His own purity. He must be given opportunity to live and express His very life in the soul and in the spirit of anyone wanting new attitudes and better, godly behavior.

The soul that is strong and sure and able to endure the slings and stones of life is the one indwelt by God Himself. Why do I say that? Simply because that is the person who is able to forgive others their faults; to overlook their omissions; to accept with good cheer the adversities of life; to forgive others who fail us and neglect to discharge their debts to us.

This is so difficult for all of us, yet it is the very question of debts which Christ dealt with. Asking for forgiveness for our own, and extending forgiveness to others for theirs. *If we cannot forgive others, then it is obvious we know nothing of our Father's gracious forgiveness to us.*

In order to be as helpful as possible in this matter allow me to mention, very briefly, three aspects of Christ's own life which can change us forever. They are the elements in His character which actually do convert our characters and control our conduct so we become like Him in the realm of our debts.

The first is His remarkable humility, expressed so clearly and forcibly in His supreme self-sacrifice. He does not sit on a personal pedestal of pride, taking umbrage at every offense committed against Him. He does not hold us at ransom for our bad behavior and our atrocious attitudes.

Instead He actually absorbs our outrageous actions in His own person. Rather than lash out at us in revenge He loves us in compassion. He longs to save us from our own dark debts.

Only as you get a glimpse of His generosity in dealing with you this way will your own tough attitude toward others ever change. You will demand your pound of flesh until the day you die in your despair. Only His grace can enable you to forgive others their debts to you.

Secondly, it is absolutely essential to see (spiritually), and comprehend completely, that Christ forgives us fully because He understands us in total. He, and only He, can explain all the complexities of our characters and our outlandish behavior. He looks on our failings, on our fickle personalities, on our wicked ways—and He weeps. He cares passionately for us as perishing people, drowning in our own despair—driven by our own sinister selfishness.

Always, ever, His cry of compassion for us is, "Father, forgive them, for in their folly and futility, they know not what they do!"

And only His life in us enables us to see others this way.

Thirdly, if we are ever to know what it means to have our own debts discharged, and in turn extend forgiveness to our fellows for their debts, this titanic transaction must actually take place in our own personal experience. It is not enough to know about it in a mere doctrinal belief. It must be an integral part of actually coming to Christ, meeting Him in person and accepting His forgiveness. This is to know Him both as my Savior and my Friend.

This is possible because He says to me in simple assurance, as He always does, "Son, your sins are forgiven!" This is such joyous good news most of us really can't believe it. Why? Because everyone else we know has always demanded that our debts be paid in full.

In a deliberate act of the will, exercising childlike faith in Him, it is possible to accept His forgiveness. This is to receive immediate release from all the rotten past that has plagued my life. It is to be set free from sin and selfishness. This is to begin a brand new caliber of life in which Christ re-creates my character and controls my conduct. He becomes the epicenter of my world.

This intimate interaction between us now empowers me, in turn, to forgive others just as He forgives me. This is to have no debts, either for me or against me. This is to be free! Free to follow Christ in contentment.

Any person who actually experiences this joyous relationship with the Living Christ in a daily renewal truly *knows Him, loves Him, enjoys Him.* This is to have darkness become light; death become life; and despair become love. It is a brand new life—Christ in me, the secret strength of my soul, the radiant joy of my spirit. Bless Him forever!

19

KEEPING COMPANY
WITH CHRIST

As our years move ahead one salient concept surpasses all others in importance. It is simply stated in the words the Lord Jesus Christ used when He was in our midst as a man. *"Follow me!"*

Various phrases for this intimate interaction between Him and us have been coined across the centuries. Here are several:

Practicing the presence of Christ.
The fellowship of God's Son.
Walking with God.
Abiding in Christ.
Christ in Me—me in Christ.
The inward journey, etc.

The list goes on and on. Some people have been a little perplexed by the various names given to this wondrous inner life of close communion with Christ. So to try and

make it easier I call it, "Keeping company with Christ."
There are seven aspects to this life which can do wonders
to strengthen our souls and energize our spirits.

1)   *He Is Here!*
     Christ is not just an abstract idea spawned by man's
imagination. He is not a fabrication indulged in by fanat-
ics. Nor is He a distant deity to whom people appeal in
times of extremity.
     He is God, very God, alive, active, at work in the
affairs of men and nations, whether they are aware of
Him or not. He can be known! He can be easily approached first hand! He can be loved! He can become the
dearest Friend! He can be trusted in calm confidence!
     He cares for us. He calls us to Himself. He chooses
us. He yearns over us. He longs to share our lives. He
gives Himself gladly to anyone who cultivates His company in sincerity of spirit and in search of ultimate truth.
His other name is *Immanuel—"God with us."* He is here!
     Christ is not just a powerful principle of supernatu-
ral proportions which controls the cosmos. He is the Suffering Savior, the Gracious God, the Supreme Sovereign
of all time whom to know is life everlasting—for we then
partake of His own eternal existence and energy.
     "Come to me, now, and here," is His generous invita-
tion.

2)   *He Encourages Us to Be of Good Cheer.*
     It is in His company that this is practical and possible
for us common people. The world becomes ever more complex and convoluted. The wickedness of men proliferates all
around us. Stress and strain, tension and turmoil are the
warp and woof of our days, and our way of life in the west.

Yet Christ comes to us amid the chaos and calmly says, *"Be of good cheer. Be strong and of good courage. Be not dismayed neither afraid!"* Why? How? When? Now and always simply because He is here. He will not fail us. He will not forsake us. He is utterly faithful. He can and does triumph over all our troubles if we will take them to Him in calm confidence, and await His good time to work them out.

This is not to indulge in self-delusion.
This is not some sort of self-hypnosis.
This is not spurious spiritism.

It is the common man or woman keeping company with the living Christ day by day.

This intense, private relationship has been the first-hand experience of millions of mortals across the centuries of our human history. It has been spoken of with awe, wonder, and profound gratitude by those who walked and talked with Him along life's way.

Without exception those who have come to know Him best are people of great good cheer and calm, quiet courage.

3) *He Invites Us to Repose in Him.*

Finding rest for our restless souls has always, ever been the eternal quest of mankind. To try and satisfy this eternal ache of the human spirit people have turned in vain, this way and that, to pursue ten thousand spurious temptations that titillated their interests.

It matters not what their souls have sought—wealth, fame, honor, sport, adventure, success, money, sensual pleasure or any other human endeavor— each turns to dust and to despair. As Solomon, who tried it all, cried out in futility, "Vanity, vanity, all is vanity!"

Composure, rest, contentment of soul have eluded men across the centuries. Why? Because men were created with an incredible capacity for communion with God Himself. And none other than Christ Himself can fully satisfy this soul thirst. Anything else is not only an illusion, but also a dreadful delusion.

That is why people can expend their entire lives in search of success in any field of purely human design and yet end up in despair and delusion. Christ asked simply, *"What does it profit a person to gain the whole world and lose his own soul?"*

All things, all achievements ultimately have to be jettisoned at death. Only the eternal values and verities in Christ endure for eternity. So it is that the individual who finds his purpose in life in Him has found the eternal panacea for his inner quest in Him. This is to come to the place of inner peace; of strength of soul; of serenity of spirit; of utter repose.

It is Christ's own presence which provides our peace, our poise, our power. It is He who dispels our fear. He is near. So all is well.

Our quiet communion with Him, and He with us, is the source of our calm confidence in Him. He composes our souls in rest. And the profound peace He provides is unlike anything ever offered by the world.

4)   *He Urges Us to Have Faith in Him.*

On the other hand Christ quietly calls us to invest our complete confidence in Himself—for everything in life. He expects us to be so sure of His steadfastness that in any crisis we too shall be the reliable people of God. We shall be those who are strong in soul, serene in spirit.

When we learn to place our simple, childlike, bold trust in Him we can face whatever comes with repose. This is because faith expels fear in life. Trust in God excludes terror. And we actually experience the calm composure and rest He offers those who rely on Him. And this can be the case for every circumstance, no matter what we face.

For this to become the great adventure of keeping company with Christ, I must also see clearly that all, all things, all events, all people are His servants. They are permitted to impinge on my life only by His good will. *They are each intended only for my ultimate benefit and for His great honor.*

This lovely view of His companionship can completely change your whole outlook forever. There will come into your everyday experiences, no matter how commonplace, a serene yet stimulating awareness of His presence. You will know then, all is well.

If, in company with Christ, you will quietly obey Him and comply with His wishes, you will be astonished beyond words what He will do. Act in simple faith and your whole life with Him will catch fire with enthusiasm.

5) *Go Out into Your World with Him.*

I did not say go into your church to meet Him. Rather, let Him lead you out into your community, into your neighborhood, into your business, into your social contacts, into your circle of acquaintances where He is not known. Dare to speak for Him. Introduce others to Him. Be very sensitive to His Spirit guiding you gently, but surely. Be brave enough to own Him openly as your constant companion.

No need to be abrasive or arrogant.

Just calmly, with deep conviction and gracious tact, let others know how you trust Him . . . and how He cares for you constantly.

There is no other way in which the presence of Christ can impact and change our sordid society except through the people of God who know Him intimately and enjoy His company. Elaborate churches; high profile preachers trying to be popular; prestigious programs; extravagant displays of human technology simply will not convince lost men and women of their deep need for Christ.

But when He is gently lifted up in honor and trust, by a strong soul who keeps company with Him, He will draw others to Himself. The world is actually looking and longing for serenity and stability amid all of its stress and strain. Christ can use you to show them where to find tranquility of soul, if you will just let Him do so daily.

Do not resist His invitation to follow Him out into this fallen, ferocious society. Go gladly, in confidence, for He is with you.

6) *Discover, First Hand, Christ's Abundant Life.*

The person who actually "keeps company" with Christ will be acutely aware that life has a keen edge to it. Daily events take on an expectancy and excitement that transcends the ordinary.

Two days ago, after devotions at dawn, I sensed an intense inner compulsion to drive about twelve miles to visit an elderly man I had not seen for months. Just as I pulled up at his gate he had come out into his garden with a chaise lounge. He was extremely weak and wanted only to stretch his aching body in the sun.

We chatted a bit about his illness; about his family; and then about the apparent futility and emptiness of his life. With sad eyes and forlorn voice he asked me bluntly, "Phillip, is your life loaded with regrets?"

It was as if he had opened wide the door to his own soul, so burdened with despair. Jubilantly I told him of the joyous forgiveness I had received from Christ for all my wayward, wilful years. I recounted how in His mercy and generosity Christ had filled me with energy and enthusiasm of His own person. "No, no!" I exclaimed. "The past with its failures had been transformed by the touch of the Master. I have met Him and He has made me whole. Life has been a stirring adventure in His company."

The old man turned gingerly and looked full in my face. "I am so encouraged to have you come and tell me this truth today!" I reached over, put my hand on his shoulder, and whispered, "He can give you His amazing life as well. Just ask Him!" For the first time his face lit up with a new and winsome light. And I was glad I had come despite the awful heat. It was the start of an abundant life in another soul seeking strength.

The simple basic issue for most of us is, "Will I or won't I promptly obey God's Gracious Spirit when He nudges me to go on Christ's behalf?" To go is to know!

7) *Just Do It! Comply with Christ's Commands.*
There is a creeping paralysis that has pervaded the church of the western world. It is the insidious idea that to comply with Christ's commands is too difficult, too demanding, too much of a discipline. This view has crept into the church from our soft, sensual, selfish culture. Christians are asked only to do that which is comfortable,

convenient and of no cost. Following Christ is to be considered only fun and games and jolly fellowship.

Yet, for the few hardy souls who are keen to keep company with Christ, there remains the ringing challenge just simply to do His bidding no matter the cost. Anything in life that is great, noble, worthwhile and enduring demands discipline, fortitude, endurance despite every difficulty. Christ calls us to follow His instructions; to comply with His wishes; just to do His bidding.

To accept His call and respond to His challenge is to find enormous fulfilment in company with Him. First because He delights to bestow His Generous Spirit upon the individual who complies with His commands. Secondly because He immediately sets us free from the prison of our own self-preoccupation to go out and run freely, gladly to accomplish His purposes. We become energetic, strong, buoyant souls who get things done for God.

Put in a nutshell the secret is, *"Whatever He asks you to do—Just do it!!"*

As I have said, across the past thirty years, to literally thousands and thousands of people all over the world, both in studies, in messages, in books, by example, *This is not legalism—this is the positive proof you truly love Christ and are unashamedly loyal to Him (read John 14, 15, 16).*

Anything else is pretense and play-acting.

To keep company with the Living Christ is to keep His commands.

His commands are not grievous but good and powerful.

They will put steel in your soul, a song on your lips, and set your spirit alight.

20

RESTING AND REJOICING IN OUR FATHER'S CARE

The theme of this chapter is one of the most challenging I know to discuss with contemporary Christians. For we live in a world where the buzzword is "business." As a society we are submerged in the false concept that the ultimate attainment is "success"—whatever that insidious word may mean, in terms of human ambitions, human activities and human attainments, using human resources.

Consequently, these concepts have swept into the church. Leaders urge their people to become involved in grandiose schemes, great campaigns, endless meetings and all sorts of impressive programs. And the majority are simply mesmerized with the idea that bigger is better.

Yet the astonishing truth is that whenever our Father undertakes to accomplish His purposes on the planet He does it through a single soul who in quiet trust reposes in Him—the person who quietly rests and rejoices in His care. There is a rest of soul to the one who truly knows God intimately. There is an amazing dimension of divine energy and strength in a solitary soul who rejoices in the utter faithfulness of our Father.

Without any foreknowledge or preprogramming, yesterday Ursula and I found the most moving documentary I have ever seen on television. It was the unadorned account of the diabolical suffering and degradation of hundreds of Dutch and British women in a Japanese prison camp in the jungles of Sumatra in World War II. To those of us old enough to recall the pathos and pain of those terrible times it was like opening once more the dreadful doors to the diabolical darkness and death that stalked the earth under the grim warlords.

But the incredible, almost unbelievable, single strand of golden glory that surmounted that cruel camp, was the life and witness of a young English missionary lady who loved music.

Purely from memory and out of her intimate life with God she could recall the music and melodies of the great hymns and fine classical music. These she put down on paper with remarkable accuracy. With the help of another gifted young woman she began to train hundreds of women, dressed only in rags, starving to death, riddled with disease, to sing the music in unison.

And the harmonies which rose in unison from those broken hearts and shattered lives became the very source of their strength and assurance of their survival. Woman after woman, now white-haired and deeply lined after more than fifty years since those nightmare ordeals, gave glowing testimony to the wonders wrought by this quiet, humble English girl who truly rested in God amid all the awful atrocities around her.

This is the sort of heroic life lived out, given up, gladly in company with God who can change the worst of conditions. As the pure, pure sounds of these great hymns and glorious music set their souls free from the atrocities of their cruel Japanese captors, those women found fresh hope and renewed strength in God.

I sat awestruck, in silence, in stillness. Tears trickled down my cheeks. I could scarcely speak—especially as I compared the purity and power of that music with the trashy, glitzy, night-club screaming that now passes for music to the Most High in some of our churches. No marvel that the "Glory of God" has passed far from among His people!

The day is fast approaching when men and women who claim to be Christians will have to make tough choices. Are they going to be part of a carnival atmosphere that caters only to phony pretense and play-acting among the churches, or are they going to find their rest and strength in God Himself?

There is a place of repose for the child of God.
There is a source of strength for the searching soul.
There is a song of rejoicing for the questing spirit.

But these are not be found in our sensual services that now proliferate all over the western world under the guise of godliness, nor in our superficial Christianity.

Repose and strength, and unshakeable confidence are to be found only in Christ's company and my Father's care! Even at the risk of being very unpopular I state this eternal truth here again without apology. The hard core, central question that faces each of us is, "Will I dare to believe God Himself can be to me all I need in this life?"

Our central problem is we do not believe Him. Most of us mouth the correct phrases and sing the sacred songs while trusting our own skills, wisdom, expertise and resources to get us through life. We indulge in duplicity, and it is an awful grief to God, besides being a discredit to ourselves.

Really nothing has changed. When Christ lived among us as a man He was dismayed at the lack of faith displayed by His own intimate disciples. We are no different. It is stated clearly: *"He could do no great works there because of their unbelief."* It was a classic case of cause and effect.

Yet there are a few of His followers who have found that when they trust Him fully, they find He cares for them completely. They discover to their delight that there is rest for the one who quietly relies on God. They enjoy a jubilant, really carefree confidence in His company. In a word they become overcomers who enjoy a dimension of life known to very few.

They are not worried by the world.
They are not depressed by despair or difficulties.
They have no fear of wicked men or evil spirits.

In this connection, one of the terrible delusions that has swept through the contemporary church is the undue prominence given to Satan. In particular, some in the charismatic movement have led millions of ill-informed people to believe Satan has the power to ravage their lives and destroy their repose in God. This is simply not so—if they truly know Christ!

The person who keeps company with Christ: Who has unflinching faith in our Father: Who submits fully to His Holy Spirit is utterly safe from Satan. Satan is a deceiver and a destroyer, but he cannot subvert the soul which rests and rejoices in God's care. Such a person is surrounded by the invisible presence and power of the Risen Christ. And Satan trembles and flees at His sight, and at His Word.

It is Christ, the Very Light of God Himself, who fully exposes and reveals the dark designs of the Deceiver.

It is Christ who in resurrection power conquers death, overcomes the forces of evil and holds Satan up to ridicule.

Christ is risen! He is alive! He, the Lamb of God, but also the Lion of Judah, reigns in honor and great power. This same Jesus the Christ shares His life, His love, His light with the person who trusts Him fully. And in that wondrous security the humble believer is safe and secure from any assault by any enemy, be it man or spirit.

Herein lies strength of soul. Here there reposes serenity of spirit. This is the secret to the songs of those who rejoice in Christ and find rest in His presence.

What I am speaking of here is not mysticism. It is the actual, everyday experience of the one who abides in Christ and Christ in him. It is the sort of serene life He intends for all His people to enjoy. But very few do!

In part this is due also to a serious misunderstanding about trouble in life. Man is born unto trouble. It is an integral part of the daily fabric of our human existence. Christ stated clearly that each day would have its own difficulties. He never said we would be exempt from trouble or tribulation as His followers. Quite the contrary! He made it plain that in this world, as we keep company with Him, there will be tribulation. But we are to be courageous, joyful and of good cheer because He is with us; He has triumphed over evil. So all is well!

It is exactly here that again thousands upon thousands of dear people are deceived and discouraged by wrong teaching. When things go wrong, or appear to go wrong, they are told they have gotten out of God's will for them. When troubles come they are told this is an outright attack from Satan, the enemy of their souls. If illness occurs they are told it is because of some insidious sin in their lives. So the long list of deception and self-delusion brings discouragement and despair to those who have never come to trust Christ completely. Little wonder so many have spiritual and temporal lives that vacillate up and down, up and down, like a child's "yo-yo."

The absolute basic belief that every child of God must come to is that if he or she lives in obedience to God's Word and in joyous harmony with our Father, *nothing can impinge on his life except by His permission.* In other words, to live in close communion with Christ is to experience daily the calm assurance of God's complete care and management of every detail in our walk with Him.

No matter if trials or turmoil come. No matter if there is trouble. No matter if there is pain or poverty. Each is for a supreme purpose understood best by my Father, but allowed to impact me for my ultimate benefit, and for His honor.

To live with this simple, profound, but childlike confidence in Christ is to triumph over our troubles and to rejoice in God's faithfulness amidst any adversity. Only then can we give genuine thanks for all things no matter what they be. Only then can we calmly rest in His special arrangement of our affairs. Only then can we praise Him with integrity for every difficulty or dilemma that may dog our footsteps.

Without going into detail, allow me to list here just a few of the sound and sensible reasons why our Father allows trouble to touch us. If you understand them you will begin to grasp the wonder of His ways with you. For all His purposes are great, good, noble and gracious toward you. Out of your trouble He can bring you lovely benefits.

1) Trouble, if properly accepted as His provision, drives us to seek Him earnestly—to find our strength in Him.

2) Tribulation is a challenge to our faith in Him. In it we discover how faithful He is to us.

3) Difficulties are designed to intensify our own intimate relationship with Him. The storm clouds are the dust of His feet walking with us.

4) In the dark valleys we come closest to Him, finding we are not forsaken, not alone.

5) The crucible of suffering pulverizes our pride, breaks up our hard hearts (tough wills) and gives us a contrite spirit.

6) The calamities of life put all values in proper perspective. Soon we see what is vain and empty—what endures!

7) Suffering and sorrow purify our personalities. Our characters become beautiful and winsome as we en-

dure difficulty with His presence recreating us in love and patience.

There are other good reasons. But these are sufficient to show that in all situations it is possible to rest in His care. No matter what comes we can rejoice in His lovely companionship.

This tremendous theme finds its most majestic expression in the thundering language penned under the inspiration of God's Gracious Spirit:

". . . We know that all things work together for good to them that love God, to them who are called according to His purpose . . . In all these things we are more than conquerors through Him that loved us. For I am persuaded that neither death, nor life, nor angels, nor principalities, nor powers, nor things present,

> *Nor things to come.*
>> *Nor height,*
>>> *Nor depth,*
>>>> *Nor any other creature,*
shall be able to separate us from the love of God, which is in Christ Jesus our Lord."

(Romans 8:28 and 37-39)

To actually know and live out these truths in the crucible of our day-to-day companionship with Christ is to partake of His strength for our souls, His assurance for our spirits.

This is to rest in Him.
This is to rely on Him.
Not just for peace and repose but also for the surging struggles and tough times when we stand strong and

calm and unafraid amid the turmoil of our times. We, like Elisha of old, should be able to cry out to our contemporaries amid the chaos of our culture: *"Fear not! For they that be with us are more than they that be with them!"* O Lord, open their eyes to see!

21

BE STILL: BE STRONG

The title of this chapter may seem to be a contradiction in terms to the reader. For we in the western world have been completely convinced that intense human activity is the secret to success. We have been told that to struggle and strain is the way to progress. The contemporary saying, *"No pain—no gain,"* is on everyone's lips.

This concept has swept into the church. It has become the main preoccupation to have endless programs, high profile speakers, colossal conventions, up-beat music with bands, drums, even hard rock rhythms, anything to assure the audience they are being well entertained.

The thought that God is very impressed with all our noise, our cacophony of clapping, laughing and carnal sensationalism has gripped the public imagination. So some readers may choose not to read this chapter at all. They may be quite satisfied to believe that it is the stirring music and the sensational services that strengthen their souls . . . not stillness in the presence of The Most High.

Several weeks ago Ursula and I attended one of the largest and most active churches in this area. To our dismay there was not even a semblance of worship in the sanctuary. People giggled, whispered, came and went as if it had been a local Saturday morning farmer's market. Odd little groups did their "thing" on the platform, even acting out a beach party in swimwear to attract attention. After some thirty-five minutes of such commotion we just walked out quietly and drove home.

Several days later the pastor phoned to ask why we had left. My simple reply was that we came to church to worship God in reverence and awe. We also came expecting to hear from The Most High in stillness and in truth. His response was that his people no longer wanted the service to be "church-like." They were more eager to have a comfortable contemporary activity in its place.

So what is stated in this final chapter may be unpopular. It may even be regarded as retrogression in our fast-paced world. But it may be used by God our Father to help the reader discover that one of the supreme spiritual secrets for strength of soul lies in being still in the presence of the Lord.

One of the greatest obstacles to entering this inner attitude of utter stillness is the notion that somehow it is a form of subtle mysticism. Or as some people call it with strong disdain, "pietism" or even "quietism." Nevertheless, no matter the charges against it, the truly great and noble saints of God, all through the ages, have discovered it to be a source of spiritual strength and inspiration as they communed quietly with the Living God.

For purposes of simplicity and easy understanding I shall here explain why stillness is so essential for spiritual well-being. It is dealt with under seven distinct aspects.

1) *Great, Noble, Creative Endeavors Emerge in Stillness.*
We need only pause quietly and contemplate the amazing majesty of the created universe to see that it was designed in stillness; that it is sustained by the power of God in stillness; that it progresses with awe and wonder in stillness.

It is the stillness of dawn and sunset; the stillness of the woods; the stillness of a mountain meadow; the stillness of a desert night under shining stars; the stillness of grass and rosebud adorned with silver dew that speak to the deepest springs of the human spirit. In wilderness, in wide skies, in a quiet garden the stillness and splendor of our Father's presence impacts our souls with purity, power and inspiration.

We then in turn, uplifted and energized by that quickening of spirit which comes from Him, in turn create that which is noble and enduring. It may be great art, great music, great literature, great architecture, great ideas, great inventions.

Their source is the Person of the Living God
who conveys to us mortals some of His eternal
essence in stillness. Be still and know that I am God!
(Psalm 46:10)

And those of us who work in sublime stillness, acutely aware of the hovering Presence of the Living God, know full well our endeavors are not our own. They originate with Him. They emerge from the deep wellsprings of His Spirit who inspires us to noble service and enduring beauty.

2) *In Stillness We Hear Christ Most Clearly.*

Truly to "hear" the voice of the Most High communing with us is not a matter of receiving auditory sounds with our ears. To "hear," in a biblical sense, is to be acutely aware within our spirits that God's Gracious Spirit is imparting truth to us. This truth is based upon God's Own Word. It has been revealed to us in the majestic Person of His Son. It is applied clearly to our conscience through the agency of His Spirit.

The individual who truly desires to hear from God must get alone with Him. He needs to be utterly still before Him, fully expecting in forthright faith to hear from Him. What then follows is a profound, powerful, but private inner conviction as to what should be done. The ancients used to call this "The great *ought* of God." It is what I *ought* to do or *ought not* to do.

Having heard Christ communicate clearly within the soul, one must then comply promptly, boldly, gladly. This is "to hear," it means to obey in calm confidence and unshakable faith. He will speak to us in stillness. We must comply without delay or debate. This is to do God's good will in openness.

What I am speaking of here is not spurious or sentimental self-delusion or self-hypnosis which becomes increasingly common. Nor am I advocating the sinister sort of transcendental meditation whereby people desire to communicate with false spirits, often believing they have heard from God. This is dreadful deception!

When we are truly seeking truth, guidance and

strength from our Father He conveys them to us through His Word, in His Son, by His Spirit. But He does it within us in stillness and surety of soul.

3) *Be Still and Wait upon God's Time.*

Too many twentieth century Christians are "busy beavers." They hustle and bustle about in a feverish frenzy of endless activities. They are absolutely sure the ultimate measure of godliness is to be busy, busy, busy, for the Master.

It is so easy for any one of us to become so involved in service that we give it greater consideration than our Savior Himself. Then we wonder why we become worn out or burned out. Yet all the time He stands quietly beside us waiting patiently for us to give Him the time He deserves, and longs to share with us.

We are an impatient people. We want prompt action. We demand instant results. We insist on a quick fix. We don't want any delays!

Then we wonder why so often there is no harmony between God and us. We pray for action on God's part, then feel betrayed if nothing happens overnight. We become tense, strained and impatient of soul—simply because we have not learned to be still in spirit and wait upon God's time.

He takes a hundred years to grow a sturdy Sequoia in the forest. We want Him to mature our characters in a week of special meetings. He patiently shapes a mountain range in fifty centuries of climatic changes. We expect Him to alter the contours of our culture in two decades.

If we will just be still and wait patiently for Him we will possess our souls in peace. He has His own wondrous ways of accomplishing things in the best time for each of us.

A superb sense of wellbeing, a calm assurance of quiet repose, a profound strength of soul comes to the child of God who waits upon God's time. The supreme secret is to be still and center our confidence in Christ. He, too, delights in these quiet interludes with us.

4) *Be Still to Watch God Work in His Way.*
In the same way that it is essential to be still and wait upon Christ to accomplish His best purposes in His own appropriate time, so it is necessary for us as His people to be still at times and watch Him work. Perhaps the single greatest mistake most of us make in our service for Him is to be so preoccupied with our own plans and programs we neglect to *see His part.* Yet His is by far the most important work.

It is fitting that I be faithful, diligent and loyal in any responsibility He entrusts to my care. But long ago I learned that beyond this it is also my humble and honorable duty to stand aside and stand still to see the astounding things He can accomplish. In so doing my spirit is ignited with an incandescent flame of bright faith in Him. My entire soul—mind, emotions and will—is stirred and strengthened in the acute awareness of His power and His might, despite all the adverse difficulties.

> *As of old Christ is accomplishing great*
> *achievements for us. "Moses said unto the people:*
> *'Fear ye not, stand still, and see the salvation of the Lord'"*

(Exodus 14:13).

It takes time to be still and actually watch Him at work. It calls for a conscious, quiet, inner act of my will to still my active mind, to still my surging emotions, to still my will so that He controls my choices and He determines my decisions. Then it is He who lifts my attention from the circumstances around me. And, in His own gracious way, He enables me to see *"The chariots and horsemen of God all around me."*

No longer do I just see a weary old world all awry. In stillness I see the wondrous work He accomplishes in that world. *Bless His name!*

5) *In Stillness Christ Draws Close.*

As a mature man, well into the sunset years of my sojourn here, I give it as my personal testimony that it is the acute, intense awareness of Christ's presence that sustains me in great contentment. In stillness He draws so close. There are moments of communion with Him which are so precious they cannot be described in ordinary words. His people have often found there is only wonder, awe and adoration that pour from us in these intimate encounters.

I do not pretend to be a pious person. I can make no claims to super spirituality. As I have said so often, I am a rough-hewn, common man, on the common road. But equally forcefully I am not ashamed to declare that I have met the Master at a thousand turns in the trail. And, His touch has transformed the circumstances and made me whole in every way.

It is to Him I turn again and again. He is with me! He is here! He is very near! He is so dear! Almost invariably the full impact of His person is most intense as I am still and quiet within. His presence is as palpable as the air I breathe, as sure as the very soil upon which I walk.

Let me say once more without apology or embarrassment: *"To know Christ as my closest Friend, to know God
as my caring Father, to know His Gracious Spirit as my
constant Counselor, is to know eternal life!"*

This intimate, close, dynamic relationship is the very
elixir of life. It is the source of quiet repose, enduring hope
and on-going contentment amid the chaos of our culture.

Just His presence brings peace.
So all is well with my soul.

6) *Be Still and Truly Worship Him Who Is Worthy.*

The Quakers, now called Friends, were well known
for their unusual form of worship in which stillness of
soul before God was of primary importance. The sanctuary was called "The Meeting House," not because one
came there to be with other believers, but to indicate this
was where one met with God in worship and adoration of
great depth.

These same devout people had a much-used phrase
to describe the sort of services common in our churches
now, *"creaturely activity."* This denoted those superficial
and sensual activities of the natural man which are not of
the Spirit, but pass for praise services.

Christ Himself stated plainly that those who come to
Him in utter sincerity of spirit, had to worship Him in
spirit and in truth. And this is done most effectively, not
in creaturely activity but in quiet contrition. It is not by
the clamor of the crowd, or the flaming displays of our
powerful programs that we truly are touched by God. His
touch comes when His still, small, personal voice speaks
to us in the still sanctuary of our own spirits, bowed
before Him in reverence, wonder and awe.

Then it is we discern something of His might, His majesty, His grandeur and His grace. For the soul this is a purifying interlude. We are stunned, amazed and overwhelmed with gratitude and absolute humility. As with the angels who surround His person we cry out, *"I am undone and unworthy—but worthy is the Lamb of God—praise and honor and glory belong only to Him."*

Living, vital encounters of this caliber cleanse our souls, energize our spirits and reshape our conduct. For in stillness we have had a glimpse of the Glory of our God. And we are made glad—glad to belong to Him.

7) *Be Still So the Dew of Christ's Refreshment Can Restore Your Soul and Rest upon Your Spirirt.*

Just yesterday it come home to me with great force that almost every family we know faces formidable perplexities. At no time in all of my long life have so many people appealed to me for help; for guidance; for support; for prayer to endure the diverse difficulties that confront them in our confused and complex world.

There is deepening despair. So many struggle with the fever of life. They are gripped with fear and foreboding of the future. They are worn and weary with the strain and stress of our sin-driven society.

Where are they to be restored, renewed, refreshed?

This entire book has been written to turn your weary footsteps toward our Loving Savior who waits for you to come to Him. He longs for you simply to settle down quietly in His presence and be still before Him. Find your rest, your renewal, your refreshment in His company. Let the still dews of His own Spirit settle down softly upon your soul.

This was what Mary did and He changed her life.
   Martha was too busy, too active—and missed His
      best.
   You are wise to accept His invitation to be still.

This is not always easy or simple to do. Some will consider you strange and even "far out." But that is a small sacrifice to make in order to find sublime satisfaction of soul in communion with Christ. This is to drink deeply of His very life.

Then you, in turn, will become a buoyant, brave soul out of whom run rivers of refreshment to those around you. You will be a benediction to a broken world in despair. Because your strength of soul and serenity of spirit are in fact *Christ in you and you in Him: the supreme secret to life.*

Other books by
W. PHILLIP KELLER

God Is My Delight

In his 35th Christian book W. Phillip Keller examines his own personal relationship with the Trinity—God the Father, God the Son, and God the Holy Spirit—and shares his insights with those who are on the same spiritual journey which he has traveled. Looking back over his own eventful life, Keller leads the reader into a deeper desire to know the Lord as Father, the Son as Friend, and the Holy Spirit as Counselor.

3051-8   hardcover   252 pp.

Joshua: Mighty Warrior and Man of Faith

The author of *A Shepherd Looks at Psalm 23* provides a captivating look at Joshua, the successor to Moses and conqueror of Canaan. Keller examines the man and his mission and provides practical insights for everyone facing the conflicts and pressures of modern life.

Readers will be motivated by Keller's challenging message—"Let us always be ready to accept any new challenges given to us under God. Let us keep on the move with Him. Do not stagnate spiritually. Be bold enough to take new territory with Christ."

2999-4   paperback   184 pp.

Sky Edge: *Mountaintop Meditations*

Written following the death of his close friend, W. Phillip Keller leads all who face the struggles of sorrow and pain back to the mountaintop of God's loving and healing presence. In quiet interludes on remote ridges against the edge of the sky, Phillip Keller takes his readers apart from the crush and commotion of our culture to experience real communion with God.

3052-6   paperback   208 pp.

Wonder O' the Wind

Wonder O' the Wind, W. Phillip Keller's richly textured autobiography, has already thrilled readers by the thousands. Now Kregel Publications has the privilege of reissuing it as a companion volume to the author's popular spiritual autobiography, *God Is My Delight.* W. Phillip Keller—author, naturalist, agriculture specialist and wildlife photographer—tells the gripping story of his life and God's loving but abrupt intrusion into his self-centered plans. He relives his trek back to Africa and eventually around the world in God's service. A vibrant love for life, for God, and for His world pulsates through this fascinating story.

2998-6   paperback   248 pp.

Songs of My Soul: *Daily Devotions from the Writings of Phillip Keller*
—Compiled by Al Bryant

For more than thirty years, Phillip Keller has thrilled readers with a rare combination of spiritual and biblical insight coupled with a celebration of natural beauty at the edge of sky and sea or in the midst of forest and field. Now, excerpts from his many books have been compiled into a beautiful daily devotional that reminds his many readers of the grandeur and goodness of God and His creation and of the variety and scope of our spiritual riches in Christ. Al Bryant has selected many of the most beautiful and helpful passages from Keller's writings for our daily inspiration.

2995-1   paperback   256 pp.